GUTTER KID

KETA LOREN

Table of Contents

Authors Note

This memoir is based on my life's experience. Some names have been changed or omitted and some events have been compressed.

Chapter One

VENTURA YOUTH CORRECTIONAL FACILITY (VYCF) CAMARILLO, CA, NOVEMBER 2007.

The bleak of the morning peeked in faintly through the narrow slit of a single window. The wire mesh glass was encased in rusted steel and centered in the staggered dingy white brick of a dimly lit cell. If you were lucky, the only time you saw one of these would be on a TV show while clogging your arteries with trans fat from the comfort of your couch. However, I never did have much in the luck department.

This 8x8 lockbox had been my home for the past nine months. A metallic jangle of keys filled the eerie stillness of the facility as the CO paced the hall doing the 0600 count, same as they did every hour, on the hour. I was barely wiping the sleep from my eyes when the roving officer on graveyard shift passed over the pane of the wicket with a flashlight, acting as a remote, changing the channel from my dream and snapping me back into my hellish reality.

The flashlight was an unnecessary evil, in my opinion. There was already a not-so-night-light in each room that reflected off of the pewter toilets from sunset to rise. Something about people committing suicide.

Go figure, you put kids in cells for years, they don't like being alive so much. Shocking. The last time someone was allowed to cover her head with a blanket, she ended herself under its cloak. From that day forward, heads were to be uncovered at all times.

You *could* cover the plexiglass casing in wet toilet paper, which would dry into something of a paper machete barrier, but it was a risky game. If you got caught covering your night-light, it was a level 3 write-up and it was an infraction that would follow you into the parole board room. I don't know about you, but making a night-light a shade less bright didn't seem like a good enough reason to stay in jail any longer than I had to. But, I had the rare commodity of deductive logic—also known as common sense—that didn't frequently grace my counterparts.

I typically resorted to using my waist-length chestnut locks as a makeshift eye mask, wrapping it around my face and securing it under the weight of my head. It blocked out the blaring light just enough that I fell fast asleep when I could get away with it. Nevertheless there was always that one cop who policed as if he got incentives for making my life hell, and every so often, he'd come and shake the door to my cage at three in the morning.

"KUNS ... *KUUNSS* ... Uncover your face!"

Overkill. *You can see my chest heaving with breath, super cop, but good work. Gold star for you.* Every thought I had toward these power-tripping ego maniacs dripped with disdain. Not all of them were bad, but you give people the power to lock other humans in a cell and submit at your every whim, it becomes something of a recipe for disaster. I had a theory that the only people who became corrections officers were the kids that got picked on at school. Had we been out in the real world, I could've beaten the brakes off of most of them in a fair fight. But this wasn't a fair fight.

I was in the California Youth Authority.

I was an inmate and they had the keys.

Every morning it was the same shit, different day. I'd awaken from a dream into the living nightmare that I could only escape by falling into yet another dream at the day's end. Sometimes I would dream I was free. Sometimes, that I had escaped.

Escape dreams were spent in a panic trying to get back to my cell before count, where they'd realized I was missing and another ten years were added to my sentence.

Ten years.

That was the minimum confinement time for escaping a maximum-security prison and though I was first committed at the young age of fourteen, maximum security is exactly what this was. I lived for the few dreams where I'd realize escaping was impossible and become lucid. It was in these that I'd take control of the dream. Transported to a time long before becoming a child prisoner, I'd sit wiggling my bare toes in the grass, stare up at a cloudless sky—and taste freedom—before inevitably waking up.

That was the thing about dreams though. You always woke up.

I tried to shake off my dread as I brushed my hair out of my face and looked around for some semblance of pants. I had just pulled the drawstring of my oversized sweats, securing them at my hips when the morning announcements came over the loudspeaker accompanied by the sharp bark of feedback.

"Breakfast in five minutes, be at your door ready or you will be written up, Breakfast in *fiiivvveee* minutes, be at your door ready or you will be written up."

They always repeated everything around here as if we were deaf. Deaf or stupid. I never could decide which was more insulting. I quickly brushed my teeth and waited with my head against the door for the unlocking of the cells to begin.

9

There were twenty-five doors on each hall and they always started at the back, unlocking one door on each side of the hall at a time in a zigzagged motion.

Always keep the inmates on one side of you.

Never let them surround you.

There were protocols.

"Neighbor."

I heard my neighbor whisper from the crack of her door. We all had nicknames for each other. Kind of like one big fucked up dysfunctional multicultural family. Most of us didn't have families so we craved the resemblance of one. Bunkie, sister, neighbor, homegirl, whatever fit. I picked my heavy head up off of the frame and grunted in reply.

"Neighbor, can you bring me some toothpaste? I'm out until canteen."

"Yes, neighbor ..."

"I'll get you back at canteen, I promise."

She wouldn't.

Like myself, she didn't have anyone to put money on her books. Either way, it didn't matter. It was just toothpaste and I was one day and a wake up away from my parole board hearing.

If you're wondering if the state provided toothpaste, that's kind of a trick question. Legally, yes, they gave us a tube of something they labeled as toothpaste. But the clear greenish gel that filled those tiny tubes was not fucking toothpaste. Your mouth would taste worse after brushing than before, it was more of a film than a paste and in my humble opinion, it was not fit for human consumption.

The morning staff's steel-toed boots shuffled across the floor as she swung the cell doors open and slammed them closed one by one. Each inmate would line up in silence by their door, half zombies from Seroquel hangovers.

Seroquel.

It was the drug of choice around these parts. Not only did the psyche write it willingly in excessive doses but, it allowed for a full ten hours of unconsciousness. In prison, any time spent unconscious is a good use of time. It was prescribed to me of course, I just refused it because I was informed. It was an antipsychotic and the average weight gain was around forty pounds. Why they were using one of the most potent psychotropics for a sleep med was beyond me. Either way, I told them they could fuck right off.

The heavy door creaked as it swung open in front of me and I staggered slowly into the hall and positioned myself with my back against the wall. Ms. Robinson made her way down the hallway unlocking until she reached the end of B Hall and shouted the same line she did every morning as if it were Groundhog Day.

"Single-file line on silence. Single-file line. *ON SILENCE!*"

We get it. We heard you the first time, you broken record.

A familiar frown had settled into my brow. She wasn't so bad. Actually she was one of my favorite staff, but it was morning and after over 275 days of this shit, you get a little bitter. We made our way to the chow hall and sat down in a not so orderly fashion. But what do you expect? It's prison. Not the military.

"Dog groomers, get your trays."

That was me. I had gotten a job at the vocational school where we learned how to groom dogs as a part of our rehabilitation. I don't know what they expected us to rehabilitate by bathing canines but I liked dogs and it paid the best. I was pretty good at it too. The highest paying dogs were poodles and only a few of us were artistically inclined enough to manage the perfectly round poofs and I had mastered the art of the notoriously elusive puffball. It was more about symmetry and blow-dryer angle than an actual talent but hey, recognition of any skill of any sort was in short supply around these parts so I'd take what I could get. We left before the rest of the population went to school so we had a priority over a few small things. One being breakfast and morning meds, the other being showers when we got off our shift.

It was the little things that got you through the days here.

I passed off the toothpaste to my neighbor as I got up to get my tray.

"Kuns."

Ms. Robinson's raspy voice filled the silence only joined by the shuffling of feet in the chow line.

"Now I know I did not see you pass something to Miss Hernandez in my kitchen; it is too early

for your bullshit."

"Ms. Robinson," I replied, attempting to hide my irritation, "it's toothpaste. Chill."

"Uh-uh, you know the rules, and don't tell me to chill, child, you know better how long you been here and this ain't ya first time! So, don't be actin' brand new—you lucky you going to board tomorrow, I oughta write you up."

I knew better than to argue with Miss Robinson. She had a lot of sass but most of it was just that. She'd talk some shit to you but she had a good heart. Most of it was bark to keep a reputation of being one "not to be played with," to hear her tell it. Ms. Robinson was all of five feet four with caramel skin and freckles on her nose. She wore her braided hair the same way every day for the last five years I had known her in my on and off incarcerations. Piled on top of her petite head with a pair of sunglasses propped up against the big swirly bundle of midnight locks.

I got my breakfast of boiled eggs over burnt toast and a tiny box of Kellogg's cornflakes and made my way back to the steel table that was bolted to the floor. They liked to bolt things to the floor here. I don't know if it was because people like to throw things or because we had a predisposition to theft, but stealing or throwing a five-hundred-pound table both seemed highly unlikely in any regard. Ms. Robinson waited for everyone to get their trays before she made her way over to my table. I was sure I was in for another lashing but she sat down quietly across from me, took a deep inhale and raised her eyebrows as if she were expecting a response from some unanswered question. I looked at her and then looked around the room cautiously before letting my gaze float back to her.

I had the habit of sitting with my back against the wall in the chow hall.

And the day room.

And—pretty much everywhere else.

Once you've been "rushed" from behind a few times, you wise up. Self-preservation in a place like this required skillful observation. I leaned back on the cold stone and set down my spork with a sigh.

"She didn't have any toothpaste, Miss R. I'm leaving and you know her family doesn't send her any money—"

"That is not my problem, Ms. Kuns."

She oozed attitude with every word.

"But, that is also not why I sat on this cold-ass seat. I could've told you *that*—from over there."

She took a quick pause to point toward the "over there" she was emphasizing.

Confusion must've quickly passed over my face because she continued without a response from my end.

"I talked to your counselor."

"Yeah," I mumbled through bites of stale cornflakes, "and ..."

"It's not looking good for your parole hearing tomorrow."

She searched my gaze for emotion or alarm, but I didn't have any to offer her.

"Yeah, that's what she told me, but I'm not gonna have a board hearing with you yelling my business across the chow hall, Miss R. Somebody's gonna smoke my date."

"Oh, you're a regular comedian, huh, Kuns?"

I loved how she said Kuns. Almost a croon to it as if she were singing my name. She almost let a chuckle escape but caught it so that it came out as a sort of scoff snort.

"Who gone smoke your date, Kuns? *Hmm?* Oh what ... in the two days I was off, you all of a sudden got beef now ... *huh?* You been doin' the same thing since you got back here nine months ago. You get up. You work. You come back, lock yourself in your little hole whicha notepads, don't hardly talk to nobody, don't even come out to program. You're like a *square* peg, in a room fulla *round* holes. *You don't belong here, Kuns.*"

"Funny, you say that in the same breath as you telling me my board hearing isn't looking good."

"It was a different breath. I'm pretty sure it was more than one breath," she replied in her true smart-ass fashion accompanied by a wink.

I shoveled more cornflakes in my mouth to buy myself some time between now and the inevitable disappointment that was sure to follow.

"You sure are quiet for it being you. You always got something to say. What? Already heard the news?"

"No, but no news is good news," I quipped.

"Stop being a smart ass."

"I'm not! They don't know what's going on! Nobody ever knows anything! And now with this new SB-81 being passed, nobody knows their

14

head from their asshole so, I'm just hoping for the best and bracing for impact—pretty standard practice—I took the course and got the certificate. It's pretty much how to be an inmate 101. So, I don't know what you want me to say."

Ms. Robinson stared me down for a moment before her stern gaze melted into one of compassion.

"You don't have to be so tough all the time, Kuns; this has to get at you on some level."

"Honestly, Ms. R—I'm just trying to eat my breakfast. I really appreciate the attempt at preparing me for more bad news but news flash: *It's always more bad news.* I'm used to it. I can handle it, cuz if I can't, then what the fuck am I supposed to do? I'm not being given options here—it just is what it is and it's not anything until I go into that boardroom and they tell me one way or the other. I did my time. I'm a model inmate. If they keep me here longer because I have a shit placement plan, then what? Are they gonna come up with a better one? No. There isn't a better one. I'm fucked. But at least I'm off parole."

Miss Robinson sighed as I took the last bite of my now soggy cereal.

"Well, I can't argue with facts."

"No … you can't."

Ms. Robinson started to stand up with an air of defeat, and as she did, I reached my hand across the table and placed in on hers. Typically, you weren't supposed to touch the correctional officers, but it was a moment and I went for it.

"Thank you," I said in a slight stammer looking up at her with an expression of appreciation that didn't commonly grace my face these days.

"Thank you for caring."

"Trust me, Kuns. I tried to not but … damn. I just …" She couldn't even make out the words explaining her disappointment in the system.

I nodded as if to say, "I know," before our gaze broke and she made her way back to the head of the chow hall and began excusing tables to dump their trays and make their way back to their cells.

SB-81 was a new law that had just been passed, making all nonviolent offenders jurisdiction of their county of commitment and not the state. The problem with that was we were all juvenile offenders. So there was no county jurisdiction on us anymore. The state had found a loophole to cut funding of parole resources to anyone who was over the age of eighteen but still incarcerated by the state under the previous law. I looked at it like a double-edged sword. On the one hand, I didn't know what the fuck I was going to do, no family to turn to and no idea how to function in the real world, let alone succeed—and on the other, for so long, this was what I prayed for.

Not having some sort of state-appointed officer and incarceration being hung over my head for the first time in almost a decade.

I spent the day in a haze.

Robotically grooming irritable, decrepit Shih Tzus with hilarious underbites and placing tiny ribbons in their fur in an attempt to distract from the ugly. My mind stayed busy recirculating the exact verbiage I was to use in front of the same parole board that had revoked my parole, and just three-quarters of a year earlier. The time passed as it always did but today, it felt like each minute lasted a week.

They call it short-timers. My entire sentence went by faster than that last day.

The inmates will tell you early on not to keep a calendar.

The easiest way to go crazy in confinement is to pay attention to the time.

Do the time, don't let the time do you was common rhetoric, and if you knew what it meant, it was very helpful information. It meant forget

16

about getting out. This was your world now, and one day you would wake up and it would be time to go but until then, the outside world doesn't exist.

Except a day before your parole hearing. That day, getting out existed very much.

And that day ... was today.

I could almost hear the clock ticking slower and slower, mocking me. Even the chaos of hairdryers and barking balls of fluff couldn't drown it out.

Tick. Tock. Tick. Tock.

I shook the thoughts from my head as Marnie walked over to my table.

The tables were about waist height with a small pole that extended upward a few feet brandishing short leashes. This was where we did all of the grooming after the bath. It helped to have the little Bingos and Scouts tied to something during the whole ordeal. The clippers were loud and frightening, and even the sweetest of pups took on the role of Cujo when it came time to cut their nails. I was finishing up my Shih Tzu when Marnie slid a ticket across the table.

"Poodle just came in ... you want it?"

Marnie was the teacher of the dog grooming school.

She was a short, butch blond woman who had obviously spent a lot of time soaking up the sun. Her face was like worn leather and stood out in contrast to her graying flax locks. She was an interesting bird. Never saw her yell or get frustrated in the eight months I had been grooming. I often thought about what her life was like outside of VYCF. She owned two red nose pit bulls she would bring in for grooming from time to time, so that much we could verify, but staff members didn't often share their personal lives with us inmates.

"Give it to Rachel ... I'm going to board tomorrow," I replied in a slightly raised tone.

Her eyes opened slightly wider than her typical gaze for a moment before shrugging and nodding, having some sort of mental conversation with herself before she snatched up the slip and spun on her heels in Rachel's direction.

"Hey ... Hey, Marnie!" I called out after her.

She faced me again.

"I was wondering if I could call it a day ... I want to shower and I have to call my mom before it gets too late. They go to bed pretty early."

Marnie looked at her watch.

"It's four o'clock."

I threw my hands up.

"Yeah, I know, it's—"

She cut me off.

"No problem, Kuns ... I'll call your unit let them know you're on your way."

"Thank you!" I called after her but I doubt she heard me over the racket.

Quickly, I placed the pup in the holding cage, gathered my things and was one foot out the door when I heard—

"KUNS!"

I looked over my shoulder. It was Marnie.

"I hope I never see you again!"

I smiled.

"Back 'atcha, Marnie!"

I spun on my heels and walked out of the warehouse, sending up a small prayer to never return.

Chapter Two

VYCF, Camarillo, CA, November 2007.

Back at the unit, I had showered and was waiting in my flip-flops with shampoo in hand and a towel swirled around my freshly washed hair. I stood toes to the yellow line that circled the CO's desk, marking out of bounds, trying to get a "black phone call."

There were pay phones on the wall but my family had never accepted a collect phone call from me in the history of my existence. The "Black Phone" was reserved for emergencies and typically only your counselor could approve it.

My counselor had the day off.

Nonetheless, I made my futile attempt to sway the senior staff on duty.

"Sorry, Kuns," was Mr. White's monotone, drawn-out reply.

"I'm the only one here—and I can't leave the desk. You know this; how long you been here now?"

They loved asking us how long we'd been here. As if we could forget.

"I just—"

"Use the payphone, Kuns."

"I can't use the payphone, Mr. White. My family doesn't exact get the warm and fuzzies when I call, let alone *pay* to talk to me," I said, turning from the desk to face the payphone he was suggesting so dryly.

"You're a smart girl ... You'll figure it out."

Asshole.

He couldn't leave the desk, that much was true but in my mind, he wouldn't of if he could.

Mr. White was always a bare minimum staff and seemingly an even more bare minimum person. His huge belly hung over his wrinkled, ill-fitting khaki slacks, almost trapped inside his dreadful mustard yellow and brown polo. His lunch made a cameo on the left pocket and as unkempt as he was, it was a wonder how he had managed to keep a state job for upward of twenty years but here we were.

Asking him for air would've ended in you suffocating.

There *was* one more option.

Grandpa Jack.

I had never met Grandpa Jack. He was kind of an enigma. If you were around long enough, someone would tell you about him. Five or so years before my initial commitment, Grandpa Jack's real granddaughter was incarcerated in VYCF, but I had never met her either. Apparently, over the years, there were many girls like me who didn't have anybody to take their calls. So, Grandpa Jack offered his line as a three-way service.

Not for everyone, of course. You had to know somebody who Grandpa Jack had known for a while and they had to introduce you. Kinda like the mafia.

Bonnie was the girl who introduced me to Grandpa Jack some years ago.

Bonnie and I had violated around the same time and were from the same area—Norcal. There weren't too many girls from Northern California in VYCF so we found some common ground. I happened to be one of two girls ever committed from my county.

The other was Estarra. We were committed at the same time.

Estarra had a tragic story similar to my own. Thrown around the foster care system from placement to placement, group homes, in and out of Curtis E Wetter Juvenile Hall, severe mental health issues and no family to protect her.

She was in prison now.

During her first commitment, she attacked a staff during a blind psychotic rage and then was put in county jail to await trial for felony charges of battery on a peace officer. She was found guilty and would serve a few years at Chowchilla—the notorious woman's prison in Southern California—before returning to finish out her sentence at VYCF.

I picked up the payphone, water still dripping down my neck from my wet hair, and dialed his number from memory. These were the days where you knew all of the most important numbers by heart.

"Hello?" Grandpa Jack answered.

"You have a call from 'Insert my name here,' an inmate at Ventura Youth Correctional Facility," the automatic voice echoed in my ear.

"To accept the charges—BEEEEPPPP—"

"Hey, sunshine," Grandpa Jack's voice came over the line.

"Hey, Grandpa Jack!"

My demeanor softened and my stress fell away. He had such a gentle voice, it made me feel safe. Now like I said, I had never met Grandpa Jack. I knew he lived in Gustine, a small dirt town in the armpit of California near Merced. I pictured him as a knockoff version of Mr. Rogers. White hair. Glasses. Maybe a cane. Sometimes I pictured he smoked a pipe and read Charles Dickens by the fireplace, when in reality he probably smoked Pall Malls, while drinking Natural Ice by a space heater.

21

Whatever.

He had shown blind kindness to me and so many other unfortunate kids that were lost in the system, and to me—he was a hero.

"You haven't called in a while, Kate, everything been OK?"

"I know, yes, everything is OK. I don't call often because I don't want to take advantage. You're always so kind, and I don't want to abuse your kindness, Grandpa Jack."

"How about you let me decide what taking advantage of me is? I'm a big boy; I think I can manage, kiddo."

I laughed.

Grandpa Jack had grit, that was for sure.

"You need to call your mom?"

"If you don't mind, I have my parole hearing tomorrow and just wanted to update her."

Grandpa Jack became flustered as he always did with the subject of my mom.

"I just don't understand why she can't be bothered to pick up a God damned phone call! You're her daughter for crying out loud."

"I know … they just can't afford—"

He cut me off so quick.

"IT'S A DOLLAR FIFTY A CALL. I'M ON SOCIAL SECURITY AND I CAN AFFORD A DOLLAR FIFTY A CALL!"

You could say he was protective.

He had never met me and he was more of a grandpa than any of the ones I ever had. One was nonexistent, meaning I had met him all of three times that I can recall. The last time I saw him, he was trying to "do good" and attempted to buy me shoes at a flea market. I didn't like the shoes they had there because I thought kids at school would make fun of me for having flea market shoes.

Which they would've.

Then, I would've gotten into a fight.

But, in his eyes, I was an ungrateful little shit and I got no shoes.

Then the other one.

He was a pastor who liked to parade us around church twice a year then returned us to live in squalor with whichever parent wasn't completely losing their shit at the time. When they came to get us, they forced us to cut our hair into hideous styles and dressed me and my two sisters in matching fruit-covered outfits. Then, after the week, it was out of sight, out of mind. They knew things weren't "*going well*" with our parents but they didn't ever feel the need to step in and rescue us either.

Maybe they thought their prayers were enough. They did have a direct line to God as they saw it. I saw it as they had all of the resources to help us and they turned a blind eye.

We were not their problem.

Grandpa Jack dialed my mother's number and we both listened to the phone ring multiple times. An anxious chill ran up my spine, as it always did before I called my mom.

I so desperately wanted her love still.

Even though she was a dry well, it seemed I never stopped sending my bucket down in hopes that one day there would be enough for a drink of water, but it was more of a desert mirage than anything. Not by fault of her own. She had her own scars and stories to tell. When you put it all together, it made sense in a very sad way. But when you're a kid, nothing would ever make sense as to why you weren't enough to receive what you saw other kids get so easily.

"Hello," she answered.

"Hey, Mom ..."

There was a pause on the line.

"It's Katie ..."

I once had a dream that I showed up at her house after being released and she didn't recognize me. I was in jail, so formally translating the dream was out of the question, but to me it meant she didn't know me.

I always feared that she just didn't know me and never would. Imagine looking at your child and thinking, "*Who the hell is this?*" That's how she typically looked at me. Like she had no clue who I was or what to do with me.

We were from different planets and it was very apparent to both of us.

"I know who it is," was her slightly offended reply, followed by more awkward silence.

"Well, I don't have much time—I just—I go to board tomorrow so you know—just calling so you knew what was going on with me."

Did she even want to know what was going on with me? Why did I call her? What was I thinking? So many thoughts ran through my mind.

"Oh, well that's good, I hope everything works out OK."

Dry. Dry, dry, dry. I can imagine she wouldn't know what to say. We always had a difficult time communicating. She managed with my sisters just fine somehow but with me, it was like everything had much more weight. She didn't want to say the wrong thing, which always led her to saying the wrong things.

Damned if she did, damned if she didn't.

Her words. Not mine.

I just assumed her life was easier without me in it so I didn't bother her much because when I did, I was typically disappointed.

"Well …"

I tried to find the words "I love you," but they kind of just swirled around my mouth before I swallowed them on second thought and replaced them with "I guess that's it …"

"Are you coming back to Red Bluff?" she asked.

"Yeah … I mean … they don't have a placement for me but they're putting me back under Tehama County jurisdiction so—I'm assuming that's what my bus ticket will say."

"Where are you going to stay?"

"I don't know, Mom."

I knew better than to ask to stay with her.

They had a beautiful four-bedroom home on a few acres of property and I was not allowed to set foot on it. I hadn't been in that house for six years. Since I was thirteen. One time, I was in a foster home around the corner from them, and I made my mom a cherry pie from scratch for Christmas. My foster-mom took me to drop it off and my mom made sure to meet me at the gate at the road. That was the extent of most of our interactions.

I had begun peeling the old yellowing paint off of the brick the phones were bolted to, reflecting my anxiety.

"Well, I hope something comes through for you, hon."

Dagger. Heart. Tears were beginning to well up in my eyes due to my abandonment issues resurfacing as they always did in conversations with her. Instead of letting her hear me cry, which would have led to me reinforcing the stigma that I was emotionally unstable, I cut the conversation off.

"Alright, well—I gotta go—I'll talk to you soon."

"OK, hon, talk soon."

I waited to hear the click of her line, signifying that she hung up, before I let a small sniffle escape.

"Kate ... you OK?"

It was Grandpa Jack. He had been listening the whole time.

I sucked up my emotions and took in a heavy breath.

"Yeah ... Ugh ... I'm alright," I replied as I swiftly swept the tears from my blushed cheeks and attempted to regain my composure.

"*I—do—not—like—that woman!*" he said with a pause for emphasis on each word before *that woman* fell from his surly, curled lips.

A statement that forced a quick chuckle through my snot.

"Well ... she's my mom so we gotta try, Grandpa Jack."

"No, I don't. You can if you like but—I hope you figure out sooner rather than later, that love don't look like that, so you can stop comparing to it and letting it hurt you this way."

Those words stung in truth.

"Well I appreciate the advice, Grandpa Jack. I appreciate everything you do."

"I might not get a chance to talk to you again, kid, but just know you're in my heart and you can always call me if you need."

He was right. He wouldn't get another chance to talk to me.

Because I would never be in VYCF again.

"Bye, Grandpa Jack ..."

I walked back to my cell in a daze, a roving staff close in tail.

Mr. White's lazy ass refused to take me to my room, so I was stuck in the dayroom waiting for a CO to come through on a check. Most people liked being out of their cells, but I just wanted to lie down. I was exhausted from the mental acrobatics of the day and sleep was my only hope for solace. I let out a sigh of relief as I heard the click of the lock and fell face-first onto my cot with an audible plop.

Laying there for a moment, I stared at the wall with the faint satisfaction that comes from zoning out. When I finally let my heavy lashes meet—breaking the trance—I shot up and grabbed the extra wool blanket that was folded at the bottom of my bed and covered myself up to my neck before wrapping my hair around my face.

Sleep … please come, I thought, sending my silent prayer to the sandman.

I was drifting.

I could almost feel it take me under when my mind swam with unwanted memories imprinted ten years earlier. I tried to come back, but it was too late. I fell into their grip as they took me like an undertow and way down I went.

* * *

GRANTS PASS, OREGON, JULY 1997.

The weather was fickle in Grants Pass, Oregon. The day before it had been overcast. Dark grey clouds with thick bellies and the threat of rain. Today, it was hot enough to fry an egg on the asphalt. We didn't care. All we wanted to do was play. Sticky handed with Kool-Aid-stained smiles. Chasing down lizards and snakes in the blackberry brush until the porch light came on.

We weren't allowed to have real pets like dogs and cats.

"They're too much responsibility."

My dad always had that line cocked and loaded.

Outside of nearly every supermarket, there would be a cardboard box full of snuggly, heart-stealing critters. The mere sight of a Free Puppies sign, would trip his alarm and—bang.

"They're too much responsibility."

He'd pull the trigger on it, as a preemptive strike, against our sure-to-come pleas.

He did allow us to have a few pet rats. A weird choice for a pet, but we weren't picky. I don't remember a time where, at least one of us, didn't have a Mason jar or shoebox with holes poked in it. Serving as home for something that would jump out at you, in an attempt at escape, anytime you would open the lid.

None of them survived and over tiny graves marked with popsicle stick crosses, we would hold a funeral.

We just wanted something to chase after that might live longer than a few weeks. Rats fit the low bar and today—we would have nine more.

"Will she have them today?" I'd ask my stepmother, day in and day out.

And, every day, she'd reply the same.

"You know, she just might!"

After ten consecutive "she just mights," I figured this might be the *she just might* that she did.

I sat in front of the cage for hours with my dirty fingernails hinged on the wire. Watching and waiting for any sign of the birth. I was always a curious kid who wanted to know everything, but everyone seemed to get frustrated when I asked why, so I learned to watch instead. After what seemed like hours, I saw a translucent sack emerge from under Baby's tail.

"SHE'S HAVING THE BABIES! SHE'S HAVING THE BABIES!"

As I ran down the hall, my excited shrieks echoed through the old barn-colored house, announcing their arrival. My sisters' feet thundered like a stampede behind me as I made my way back. We pushed and shoved, vying for a space around the cage, to watch as the bloody birth began. An hour later, there were nine squirming, ugly, pink, fingertip-looking specimens.

We all pointed and a chorus of excited squeals, giggles and ews filled the tiny room as we all tried not to barf. It was a weird combination of feelings but I didn't mind; it was exciting and I lived for anything out of the norm. The joyful chaos was intoxicating and once we were bored of the miracle of birth, we returned to play. Running around the room and swinging from the frames of the bunk beds until Christie's voice boomed from the living room.

"Alright! The baby is going to sleep! Outside—NOW!"

The room erupted with the typical unison "aw," followed by the pitter-patter of tiny feet running down the hall, through the back door and back into the wild—otherwise known as our backyard. We played in the fort we had built in the hollows of a blackberry bush as the unforgiving heat beat down on us. After an hour of make-believe, I would go in for a glass of water and when I did, I would make my way back to the cage and count again.

Nine.

Nine little pink squirmy things.

One, two, three, four ... I stopped.

There were only eight.

Alarm filled my tiny mind thinking someone had kidnapped one of our rats. I ran to the living room in a flash and dragged my stepmother back to the cage, tears streaming down my face.

"There were nine! Somebody took one! Somebody kidnapped one of our babies!"

Christy laughed as she pulled me to her hip, cradling my head in her hand.

"Awwee … sweetie … no … nobody kidnapped the baby. Mama probably knew there was something wrong with it and rejected it. Sometimes they eat the ones that are hurt or not gonna survive. It's a primal thing; it's totally normal."

I was horrified.

My mind wasn't equipped for such information.

Not that she was wrong for telling me, it was a perfectly acceptable answer, it's just that … my mind took that information and equated it with humans. Was that why my mother rejected me? Was there something wrong with me? Was I not going to survive? Humans obviously didn't eat their young so maybe rejection was the only possibility. I wanted to ask Christy but people didn't like when I asked why.

I let the sinking feeling in my stomach take me over and swallow me whole as I ached from keeping it inside. Tears fell in droplets against Christy's jean skirt, which my face was now pressed into.

"Awe … honey, it's OK … we still have eight babies. That's plenty to play with, OK?"

She tried to console me but, that wasn't why I was crying. I almost got up the nerve to ask again, then decided I didn't want to hear the answer.

What if she said yes?

I buried my face into her skirt as she stroked my head as my eyes ran like faucets until the well ran dry.

* * *

VYCF, Camarillo, CA, November 2007.

I woke up covered in sweat with tears rolling down my face, which wasn't uncommon. I'd had many a night terror. I always preferred when they were fully imaginative because they didn't pack such an emotional punch to the gut. This one had obviously been triggered by my earlier conversation with my mother. Every time this happened, I wondered why I even called her. No good came of it. But I always came back with my hands cupped, hoping she just this once she could spare a crumb. I wiped the tears from my cheeks and flopped over, slamming my fists into the thin mattress in an attempt to move the stagnant mix of rage and frustration through me quicker. Taking a nap was a bad idea. Now I was up and I had board tomorrow. I tossed and turned all night like I was awaiting the first day of school. Nervous excited. Every possible scenario fluttered through my head as I made a complete mess of my bed with all of the shifting, attempting to find a comfortable position on an inch-thin "mattress" supported by a steel frame.

I typically slept fine. I had learned how to manage even under the most uncomfortable circumstances. But tonight, it would've been impossible to sleep under the most luxurious accommodations. I was the princess and the pea, and the pea—was in my head. I was still awake when they came down the hall for 0600 count.

"Count clear, Count. Is. Clear," came the main tower's report over the loudspeaker.

Count always annoyed me. Made me feel like a number, which I was— to them at least.

#89590.

I didn't realize I had passed out briefly and woke up to Ms. Robinson swinging my door open for breakfast.

"Kuns?" she called to me in my bed. "Do you want to go to breakfast?"

31

My eyes fluttered open. Nobody had ever asked me if I *wanted* to do anything here before. She was offering me a bit of much-needed compassion.

"I didn't sleep, Miss R—is it cool if I skip it?"

"No problem," she replied with a soft smile as she closed my cell door and I quickly fell back into the slumber that had eluded me all night long.

Rap, rap, rap … Keys on the wicket.

I opened my eyes and looked for the source of the noise and saw Ms. Robinson's face peering back at me.

"You got board in five minutes, Kuns …"

I darted up out of bed. Five minutes! That wasn't enough time to pull together a presentable version of myself, but it was all I had. I quickly flew around the room, brushing my teeth and running my brush under the pressureless faucet to force some feign attempt at a neat bun. I was still thrashing around attempting to put my legs in jeans, when Ms. Robinson made her way back down the hall. My whole life I had been putting my feet through leg holes of jeans without a problem but today, it was like trying to solve some algebraic equation.

Left leg, left hole. There we go. Right leg—

I fell as she opened the door. I was flat on my back with one leg through my special order Levis and the other high in the air with a perfect upside-down view of Ms. Robinson, in a fit of laughter, leaning up against the doorframe attempting to regain her composure.

"CHILD, WHAT IN THE—WHAT ARE YOU DOING?" She made no attempt in masking the apparent hilarity.

"PUTTING ON PANTS IS HARD," I yelled back sarcastically.

"Today got you all twisted up, huh?" she said through a laugh.

"Quite literally actually," I joked as I sat up and finally mastered the simple art of dressing myself.

"Man, oh man, you crack me up, child! I am sure gonna miss you and that beautiful voice echoing through these halls."

"Don't jinx me ... we don't know what's happening yet."

"Ah nah. You gonna be just fine. If they don't let *you* out, they ain't neva letting anyone out of here ever again. You did the deed. Your time is up. Just believe it. Gone now and take a deep breath everything's gonna be alright." Her soft knowing voice sent a blanket of calm over my agitated spirit. She always knew what to say.

I took a deep breath and stepped out into the hall.

"I GOT ONE NEED A TRANSPORT TO BOARD," Ms. Robinson yelled down the hall.

The quick jingle of keys signified that a rover was already waiting to take me up to the main tower.

"I got it, I got it, thank you, Ms. Robinson." Jackson slid in between us and made no stop on his way to the back door.

Ms. Robinson waved her hand toward the exit.

"Your chariot awaits." I laughed, the nerves falling away a bit more at the sound of her beautiful sarcasm. I started for the door, only pausing for a moment to give Ms. Robinson a quick smile over my shoulder as I followed him to find out the fate of my freedom.

"YA GONNA DO JUST FINE!" Ms. Robinson called out to me. The sun touched my face and the door slammed shut behind me.

Chapter Three

VYCF, Camarillo, CA, November 2007

Waiting in the hall for board was one of the most torturous experiences of my life and I've been through some shit. In comparison to the loud ruckus of the housing units, it was eerily quiet. So quiet I was afraid the suit-donning passersby could hear the screaming of my own thoughts. The anxiety Ms. Robinson helped ease was now rebounding and causing my stomach to flip in acrobatics. My mind ran rampant. I twisted my hands around one another in an attempt to disperse the excess of nervous energy.

The click of a pair of heels echoed from around the corner and were headed in my direction. I looked toward the source of the sound just in time to see a very stern-looking woman make her way around the corner. She was dressed in a navy blue dress jacket, with obscenely large silver buttons down the center that perfectly matched her skirt. Her hair was pulled back in a neat twist of some kind and there was an air of authority that bled through eyes behind her otherwise feminine gaze. She glanced at me through her glasses ever so briefly before opening the door to the boardroom in front of me and letting it softly close behind her.

It wouldn't be long now.

A few minutes passed and the door creaked open slightly.

I could hear the mumble of voices coming from behind it. Too much time was passing with the boardroom door cracked open for my anxiety to take. With every second that passed, my heart raced a bit faster. My palms were becoming clammy and my head got louder and louder until I thought it would be the cause of my going deaf. Fortunately no one has ever gone deaf from noise inside their head. The door opened fully and a CO leaned out.

"Kuns—you're up."

I had been waiting for another inmate to emerge from the room to give me some hint of how the emotions were running on the other side of the door, even if only by reading their face—but apparently my case was the first after a brief adjournment so there were no hints or signs to observe. Typically after the board took lunch, they were in a food coma and slightly more irritated.

It was common knowledge going to board after lunch was a less predictable path. Not that you

had any say in what time your board hearing was but after year in and year out of girls coming and going from board, we had put together the patterns as best we could.

I had never heard of a "brief adjournment" before though. What were they adjourning for? Not for the last hearing. That decision had been made. It had to have been about me. The thoughts came sixty a second, relentless, as I pushed off from the metal arms of the cracked leather chair and made my way into the boardroom.

It was freezing and the flicker of the old florescent lights overhead cast a chilling shadow on the stern woman's face. A single wooden chair faced the panel that I assumed was meant for me. I sat in it quietly and shivered. Typically, there were three board members. Today there was one. I didn't know if this would work in my favor, or against it. I was at the mercy of this one human soul. She was my God and in my experience, no human should have that type of authority over another but what did I know.

I was just an inmate. For now.

"We are here to review the case of YA number 89590 for the possibility of parole. Please state your name for the board."

The board. What a joke. She was the board. I didn't say that out loud though. What I did say was:

"Katie Kuns."

"And this is your first parole board hearing since your revocation back in …" She rifled her thin fingers through my case file for a moment. The stillness of the room was deafening.

"February … is that correct?" She looked up at me with an intense gaze. So formal.

"Yes, ma'am," I replied quietly.

I learned early on, quick concise answers were the most productive. Give them the floor and all the power and you just might walk out of here a free girl.

"Well, we are having some concerns with the parole plan due to the changes in the new laws regarding county and state jurisdiction. Your success rate of integration back into society with no resources is appalling, if I'm being quite honest, and I'm having a hard time wrapping my head around allowing this nonsense. It's setting you up for failure and I don't want to stamp my approval on it."

I began to rebut, but she continued cutting off my chance.

"Especially with your history of trauma and mental illness. We have multiple diagnoses. No support system and no place of residence. I have never seen a more crap parole plan in all of my years."

She had never seen such a crap parole plan and I had never heard a board member say the word crap. So, you could imagine we were both out of sorts.

"If I may …," I plead to her.

"You may," she resigned.

"It is what it is. If you keep me here another three months, six months, whatever—I'm just going to be sitting in this chair again with that same *crap* plan in front of you and so if you don't let me out today, we're just prolonging the inevitable and I've done everything right, ma'am. I've been a model inmate. I don't get into trouble. I work and I stay to myself and if you—"

She cut me off with a wave of her hand.

"I'm not saying I'm not going to parole you …"

Another long pause filled the air.

"I'm just saying—I don't like it. Some days, we do our jobs and know we did the best we could. Other days—days like *today*—I know what I'm doing is wrong. Even if I do the right thing. That's where we're at."

"Sounds a lot like my life."

I didn't mean to say those words. I regretted them the moment they fell from my lips. I expected a glare or for her to be taken aback, but instead the frustration melted from her eyes and compassion replaced it. Only for a split second, but I saw it. It gave me relief that there were good people in the world. The world I had come to know had made it hard to believe and even when I did encounter these moments, they were always brief and so easily forgotten.

The board woman, whose name I never knew, sifted through the plan again, shaking her head.

"The date is November fourteenth, 2007. The decision of the Department of Juvenile Justice's parole board is to grant Katie Kuns parole and forego her jurisdiction under the new bill SB-81. She will be permanently discharged from parole under the authority of the State of California and will return to her county of jurisdiction, Tehama ..." She mispronounced it as everyone did. I didn't correct her. I was in shock.

"A court date is set for the twenty-ninth of December to review the county's obligation, if any, to Ms. Kuns—but most likely they will close your case."

The disappointment in her voice was alarming to me. I didn't expect much emotion on her part but I could tell she was having to hold her shit together pretty neatly.

"The state will provide funding for lodging for two weeks in ... the Crystal Motel ... on Main Street. Do you know where that is?"

Of course I did. It wasn't called the Crystal Motel because of all the meth heads that stayed there but it was kind of a Freudian phenomenon.

"Yes, ma'am, I know where it is."

"You will be given a sum of two hundred dollars and a Greyhound bus ticket to Red Bluff, California, which will be leaving tonight at eight thirty."

The words took a while to find their way from her mouth to my ears, due to my complete and utter dissociation, but they were digested in enough time that there were no visible signs of my full disconnect from reality.

I sat in the chair and stared at her like a deer in the headlights. I didn't know what to do. Was that it? Could I just get up? I decided it was best if I let her excuse me.

"You're free to go, Ms. Kuns. Best of luck to you."

Those words rang in my ears louder than all of my racing thoughts combined, nearly drowning out the fear of what I was going to do after the two weeks was up. I managed to compartmentalize it for the time being. I didn't have a choice. I mustered up the know-how to form the seemingly simple sentence, "Thank you," before I rose from the chair and floated toward the door.

I was free.

I was fucking free.

Well in a few hours I would be, but that was the same thing to me.

Jackson was waiting to take me back to my unit in the hall. I walked out, and quite obviously my face was blank because a puzzled look crossed his as he stood up to walk out the door with me toward the rover.

"Good news?" he questioned.

I took a huge breath and let out the first sigh of relief my lungs had seen in quite some time.

"Yes," I replied. "The best."

* * *

GREYHOUND STATION, CAMARILLO, CA, NOVEMBER 2007.

A lot of people ask what freedom tastes like. For me it tasted like the Marlboro Light 100 I had bummed off the first smoker I saw outside of the Camarillo Greyhound station. Nicotine filled my lungs like a hug from an old friend. Nine whole months spent wanting a cigarette and now I held it between my index and middle fingers, breathing in every sweet cloud as if it were heaven itself.

Greyhound buses are the bottom of the barrel when it came to transportation. It was reserved for the poor and the parolees. I was both. I finished my cigarette and let it fall from my fingers onto the concrete, stamping it out under my sneaker. It was time to go.

40

Talk about a train to nowhere.

There were two layovers. One in Los Angeles, the other in Sacramento. I had taken this ride a few times before. Sacramento wasn't so bad—but Union Station, for a single teenage girl at night, was questionable to say the least.

Union Station is dead center skid row and was crawling with crack-heads selling stolen batteries and bootleg DVDs. But that wasn't the worst part. It was also known that young impressionable girls—frequently runaways—were sex trafficked through there, so you couldn't sit in one place too long without a pimp noticing that you were alone. One who would attempt to finesse you into changing your plans and run away with him. I had no desire to have a pimp or sell my body, so mainly I was just terrified. But I had learned early on, that to show fear was to mark yourself as prey. The best thing to do would be to flirt, smile and charm. This would buy time to think of a creative way to get out of dodge.

It was more complicated than one might think.

Two hours passed, with my head pressed against a cool Greyhound window, before I started to see the telltale skyline. We were approaching Union Station. I shook off the slumber that was creeping up on me and started to feel around for my things. I didn't have much—a bag of old journals I had filled with songs and poems over the last nine months, but they were everything to me. I clutched them against my chest as we pulled into the terminal.

I knew the drill. Hop off the bus for two hours for it to be cleaned and refueled, then hop back on. Sounded easy enough. But the two-hour wait in the jungle that was Union Station was the tricky part. I had already begun scouting out someone to buy me a pack of cigarettes. I was of age, but no ID and I looked young. Luckily, I knew that young, pretty girls could typically get middle-aged men to do favors for them, so I worked that angle.

The man sitting next to me on the bus was such a man.

I wasn't off the bus ten minutes before I had two packs in hand. I lit up another cig and basked in the moonlight, soaking up my freedom. I followed my tired feet to a nearby empty bench, somewhat away from the chaos, sat my heavy body down, and looked up at the night sky.

I always expected to see a sky full of stars when I looked up, but only a scattered handful speckled the black. LA had its own stars. The ones in magazines that walked red carpets. I stared anyways.

I don't know how long I had been gazing up when a shadow fell upon me. A strange man was staring at me with his hand on his chin. I wished I hadn't looked down. Here came the pitch.

"OK, OK … you a fine little glass of champagne, where you from, lil' mama?"

I didn't know him but this conversation gave me a sense of déjà vu. He was incredibly attractive. Dressed way too nicely to be here taking a Greyhound bus. Not nice in a GQ way—more like a rapper. Everything sparkled from his rings to his teeth.

He was a pimp.

I knew better than to be rude so I decided to flash a smile and make nice while I plotted my escape route.

"Norcal," I muttered under my breath, before taking a drag of my cigarette.

"Oh, OK, OK! I'm from the Bay myself. People call me Green Eyes—but you could call me Daddy if you want."

He winked, followed by a smile of pure glitter. He reminded me of the Cheshire Cat from *Alice in Wonderland* with the way his cool dripped off of him. Every word was butter. Smooth and soft.

A puzzled look crossed my face but I didn't respond.

"Whatchu already got a daddy, mama?" He looked me up and down like a piece of meat. "He just left a fine piece like you out here all by your pretty self? That don't even sound right. Shit ... a man could take over the world with a girl like you!"

My head was swirling. Partially from the nicotine rush and partly from adrenaline.

I laughed a nervous chuckle in an attempt to hide my dread.

"I'm sorry, can I help you with something?" I feigned stupid, as was a common practice of mine when confronted with danger. If people think you're dim, they don't see you as much of a threat. There was a time for fight, there was a time for flight, and *this* was the time for neither.

Now was the time to hustle the hustler and it was a very tricky game.

No pun intended.

Easy—I thought to myself—*just be easy.*

I had a talent for making light of the dark spaces I encountered. I was used to it, so I was good at it. I spent the next few moments praying someone would walk by and ask if I was OK or pretend to know me, but that only happened in movies.

"It's not safe out here, baby girl. Why don't you let me take you somewhere safe. It'll be fun ... we can get to know each other." The glitter in his mouth distracted me every other word.

Yeah, it's not safe because of weirdos like you, bro, I thought to myself.

"Ahah ... no, my dad's gonna be waiting for me and I don't want him to call the cops ... he's the type ... but ... you can give me your number and I can call you when I'm back in town."

43

I didn't have a dad who would call the cops.

As a matter of fact, I didn't even know where my dad was, but he didn't know that.

A pen appeared from nowhere and he grasped my palm in his diamond fingers and wrote a ten-digit number across my hand.

"Write that down somewhere else so you don't lose it, baby."

"I will," I replied.

I didn't.

"I'm gonna go get some food before this bus boards but, it was nice to meet you ..." He could tell I was searching my mind for his name because he took the hand he had just written on and kissed it.

I shivered.

"Green Eyes."

"Green Eyes. Nice to meet you, Green Eyes."

I slowly pulled my hand from his grasp and disappeared into the station, never to see Green Eyes again. Little did I know, the next time I was in LA, I would find myself in the exact same place, under the exact same circumstances. Next time, I wouldn't be so lucky.

Chapter Four

Rivers Edge RV Park, Red Bluff, CA, New Year's Eve, 2007.

Small droplets of blood spotted the weathered linoleum floor—not my own. Daniel tried to grab my arm, but I spun out of his grasp, knocking various items off of the counter onto the floor of my single-wide trailer. My face was hot with rage and my fingernails clawed into the side of his neck in an attempt to push him out the sliding glass door.

I hope it hurt. Fucking scum.

"GET—THE FUCKKKKKK—OUTTTTTTTTTTTT!" I screamed at the top of my lungs.

Every part of my body was shaking. The hairs on my neck and arms were standing up on end and my blood was boiling, leaving my face the shade that embers glow. Swatting my unkempt hair out of my face to get one last good look at him leaving. I was livid, and honestly, it could be argued that the devil himself had possessed me. No sleep for days, out of my drug of choice and losing my ever-loving mind.

The rest of the world was celebrating as the ball dropped. I—was dropping the ball.

The irony wasn't lost on me.

I was sure the cops would be called or the trailer park manager would be around in a few to see what all the commotion was about.

"You're a fucking lunatic!" he screamed back at the trailer.

Didn't he know not to call crazy people crazy?

I snapped like a matchstick under the wheel of a Mack Truck. Before I knew what my hands were doing, they had grabbed a large crystal ashtray from off the wooden deck and chucked it at his head. I'd never had an out-of-body experience before but—as I stood staring, stunned, as the ashtray spun through the dim glow of the porch light—I watched it play out in slow motion from far above my physical body.

The regret was instant but it was too late.

It missed his head by an inch and we watched in mutual shock as it shattered on the gravel pavement at his feet. My hands didn't always have a life of their own, but once I saw red, they couldn't be trusted. Daniel spun on his heels in a fuming fury and bolted toward me. I sidestepped to safety and slammed the slider closed just as he reached it, a signature rage painted in his glowering green eyes.

A psychotic laugh ricocheted off of my protective barrier, taunting him with an expression that said *you lose*. He stood there—almost too still for a moment—before sending his boot through the glass. It didn't shatter, shockingly enough. It did, however, cave in a perfect boot print at the bottom of the door where he struck it. Defeated, he spat at his reflection, flipped me the bird and disappeared into the night.

Once he was gone and I was left alone with my thoughts, I crumbled.

Panic. Paranoia. Fear. Contempt.

I could hear my heart thumping in my temples.

You'd think it'd be the opposite, but I had built a defense system for survival. Crisis, dysfunction—that is where I thrive. Take it away and there was no one to hurl my frustration at. It was just me with me, which was, even on my best days, a lonely space to fill.

I slid down the tacky wood planks of the trailer wall—using all the strength I could muster not to collapse—curled myself into a human ball and cried.

I was coming down. Hard. From meth and adrenaline. I needed a shower, some food and a good night's sleep wouldn't have hurt me either. I wouldn't do any of these things. Why? Because before I even got up, a knock came at my door.

It was Tim.

Tim had dope.

I slid the door open to the halfway mark, which was as far as it could go with its new boot print in it.

"Yo, I just saw Daniel bolting down the stree—whoa! What the fuck happened to your door, Katie?!"

Tim spent a moment looking around at the disaster that was my home. I usually kept a decently tidy space—you know, being on meth and all—but at the moment, the trash can was toppled over on its side and broken dishes were strewn across the floor, indicating an obvious struggle.

"Your fucking dick of a cousin, that's what." I was still shaking. "Do you have any dope?"

"Uhhhhhh." He looked around the trailer once more before stepping inside. "Yeah, but … you sure you don't want to just call it a night?"

I shot him a glare that would've killed him had it been a crystal ashtray.

"You're not my fucking dad, Tim—light up or get the fuck out. It's been a fucked up night."

Beads of sweat had formed on my forehead and were now trickling down my face. I pushed them into my hairline, grasping my head tightly in my palms, as I took a deep inhale. Tim tilted his head to the side in disapproval before he replied.

"Don't come at me like that, man … I'm not the enemy here. Chill the fuck out." He rifled through his coat pocket.

"Here."

Tim shoved a glass pipe into my hands as he made his way past me to sit on the grimy sofa I had found behind a local Salvation Army. I slid the door shut and joined him, sinking into it slowly. I had drugs.

Flick. Flick. Nothing.

One more try.

Flick. The lighter was dead.

"FUCKKCKKKKKKKK!" I screamed under my breath, as I chucked the useless chunk of plastic and metal at the wall. Even with a pipe in my hand, I was a live wire perched on the edge of a couch.

Addiction is much like a little gremlin is living inside of you. When it's fed, it's happy. When it's hungry, all hell breaks loose. Your best bet is to never feed the gremlin at all. You could live your whole life not knowing it was even there. But once you awaken it, it will always be there. Waiting. Wanting to be fed, and mine—was starving.

"KATIE! JESUS EFFING CHRIST—HERE!" Tim passed me a torch.

"You smoke … I'll pick some of this shit up. Just chill the fuck out so they don't call the fucking cops, man. Neither of us need to see cops right now … Got it?"

I got it. I held the pipe to my lips and instantly, the rage fell away. *Hello, my love. I've missed you.* Smoke filled up the ball of the pipe, as I twisted it gently, waiting for it to start rolling so I could take the first delicious inhale. I filled my lungs to capacity with the vapor before slowly lowering the pipe from my face and exhaling a cloud so thick that I lost visibility of everything in front of me. I swam behind my eyelids for a moment before I brought the pipe back to my mouth. A few hits later I was seeing clearly again. (Well, as clearly as you could while high out of your gills on meth.)

Tim was sweeping up the last of the glass off of my kitchen floor before picking up the trash can to empty the dustpan. He looked around in satisfaction.

"See … it's not so bad. You're good."

"Look at my fucking door, Tim." I gestured at the boot print.

"You're fine—it's fine, look …" He opened the door to the boot print and shut it again.

"Full mobility!" He always did have a stupid smile on his face.

"Half, Tim—half."

"Whatever, man, it's not like you're some fat fuck. You can fully fit your ass—through the fucking door. That's the purpose of a door. To go through it. You can still go through it." He had begun to laugh as he slid the door back and forth.

"Open. Closed—open, closed. See? Full mobility."

"You're so fucking stupid," I said, unable to hold my grimace any longer and cracked the first grin my face had furnished all night.

"Ah, but you love me though, Katie. I fixed your house, brought you drugs, made you laugh. Come on now—what's not to love?"

It was true. I did love him. As a brother. He dated my childhood best friend, Alyssa, for a few years before going to jail the last time so, we had history.

Timmy made his way through the layers of dope fog and plopped down beside me again. He sat in a slouch, reaching his jittery hand toward me in expectation. His fingernails were rough and black from smoking dope, but he was otherwise put together.

Timmy was a character who wore his scars like badges of honor. His blond, slightly balding hair was always slicked back with what I'm sure was the same gel he had been using since high school. He was ten years older and had blue eyes that probably would've been beautiful if they weren't dilated into little black pools all the time. One of his pupils looked like a keyhole. The previous Christmas, Alyssa had left him for a street kid named Craig and they had gotten into a brawl.

Tim gave Craig a glass of Jack Daniels as a peace offering—Craig smashed the glass in Tim's face. Popped his pupil.

He still had enough vision in the eye to stare down the barrel of the pipe, which he was currently doing.

"I'm getting my settlement money," I told Tim, breaking the silence.

"Oh yeah, I heard about that—that's cool. You gonna hook your old buddy Tim up?"

Everyone heard everything in this town. People had nothing better to do and everyone was dirt poor. If word got out someone was getting a large sum of cash, the news spread like wildfire with a single intent—to latch on to the unsuspecting victim like a leech, bleed them dry of every last red cent.

The settlement money was from an accident I was in when I was thirteen. I had been racing an ATV out on some property and hit a ditch where PG&E dug a survey hole and never filled it back up. I flipped it going fifty miles per hour with no helmet. It landed on top of me, crushing everything on my right side.

I was life-flighted to the nearest ICU, where I would spend six hours in surgery as they Frankensteined my limbs back together with titanium rods and plates. The structured settlement payments were scheduled to come to me at eighteen, twenty-one, twenty-five and thirty.

But I was broke now, so I sold them. For less than a quarter of what they were worth.

"You know I got you, dumb ass," I slurred as I hit the pipe again.

The clouds always reminded me of Van Gogh, a *Starry Night* knockoff, swirling through the air. Instantly my thoughts took a turn from art to business. I looked at Tim with curiosity. I bet he would know. Even if he didn't, I wouldn't know unless I asked.

"Hey …"

"What's up?" His popped pupil eye wandered in the other direction as he attempted to make eye contact with me.

"What do you think about me flipping some weight? Do you know where I can get a few ounces?" He fidgeted with his belt buckle, hesitating as though he had to fully digest the question before he could answer.

"You sure you want to do that? You just got off parole." Quick flashes of the cells I had roamed flooded my mind's eye before I blinked them away.

"Why you always bringing up old shit?"

An involuntary laugh escaped through my teeth, his quick to follow.

"You're fucking crazy, Kate …"

"I'm aware that that's the common consensus, but I didn't ask you what you thought of me—I asked you if you could help."

My insistent sapphire eyes met his once again, awaiting his reply.

"Yeah, I mean ... it's not my guy but Ronny's got a guy ... did you ask Michael?"

Michael was my current fling. Daniel was just staying with me because I owed him a favor. Not anymore though.

"Not yet." I broke my gaze and refocused it on the boot print in the glass. "Kinda just came up with the idea—I gotta get out of here."

"Just use the money and leave," Tim replied sensibly. I didn't speak logic. All of my mental equations had a hidden number to factor in. Like a seven was stuck on my calculator. Two plus two always equaled eleven.

"You don't get it," I replied.

"Nah ... I think it's you that doesn't get it. The days of Pablo Escobar and Freeway Rick are over, dumb shit. You think you're gonna be a kingpin or something? You're a walking *Don't do drugs!* billboard, Katie," he said, shaking his head with a chuckle. "It's a dumb fucking idea."

The nerve of that man.

"Fuck you talking about, you fucking hypocrite? You've been selling dope for years."

"On contraire." He did a little wave thing with his hand, before continuing in what might have been the most atrocious French accent my ears had ever heard. "I supply the demand, *if*—the demand finds itself in my presence. *I* am not the dope man."

"First, it's *au* contraire, and second, potato patahto, bro ... but whatever helps you sleep at night ..."

"I admit nothing," he replied in the accent again, this time throwing in an intentionally coy smile.

I lit a cigarette and took a long inhale. Time passes slower in your mind on heavy stimulants such as meth, so the next time I went to take a drag, half of it was ash and the cherry resembled a glowing red Christmas tree. The ash fell from the cigarette to my pants before I could close the short distance to the ashtray.

"Fuck!" I said, wiping ash from my jeans onto the stained carpet.

"Fucking dirtbag," Tim said with a chuckle.

He reached his hand toward me as if to say, "let me hit that." I passed him the cigarette and leaned my head back on the worn fabric of my secondhand, dumpster couch. I needed to sleep. I had been up for four days and had destroyed my face in an attempt to pop pimples that in all actuality probably weren't even there.

Just a little sleep. Just for a moment. I closed my eyes and was gone.

* * *

Curtis E. Wetter Juvenile Hall, Red Bluff, CA, 1999.

Every bone in my eleven-year-old body ached in longing as I sat in an 8x8 holding room in an archaic and crumbling detention center. How had this place not been condemned? I was scared. The room smelled of vomit and tears. Foul and sad. Horror gone sour. The tears would dry on my face just before a new swell would empty onto my flushed freckled face.

Crocodile tears, they said.

As if an eleven-year-old girl wouldn't be devastated that she had just been handcuffed, taunted, and shoved into the back of a caged police car, before being brought to a cold cell, to sit for hours and hours. *Alone.* Right before they closed the steel door trapping me inside, a single sentence slipped through the crack.

"All this paperwork for a fucking runaway."

Why? Why was I running away? Surely not all kids ran away from home. Especially not at eleven. But nobody asked me that question. I wasn't a kid. I was an irritating amount of paperwork, that came in thirty minutes before they were scheduled to be off. My humanity overshadowed. I was nothing more than a defiant inconvenience.

I pulled my goose-pimpled arms in through the sleeves of my T-shirt to wrap my body for warmth. It didn't help. My chattering teeth hummed in harmony with the white noise surrounding. My mind flickered in and out. I would have done anything to fall asleep, but the conditions made it nearly impossible. I pulled the rest of my skinny limbs inside my T-shirt, curled myself into a ball in the broken lawn chair and rested my forehead on my knees.

Fetal position.

Every time I closed my eyes, I saw him. Rage in his eyes. Mine bulging, begging for breath. My tiny hands clawing at the giant calloused ones around my throat. Did he feel my tears on them? Did he notice his hand wet as he tried to strangle a child? Dirty sneakers, dangling, kicking. My thirteen-year-old sister grabbing a knife. I couldn't hear her words. But he could. Vision going dark. Kicking. Clawing. *Please no.* I'm going away now.

Black.

I gasp awake.

Why? Why was she running away? You'd think they'd ask that question.

Chapter Five

The next few months came and went in a drugged-out blur. I had been kicked out of the trailer park for extensive "suspicious activity," which I knew was coming, and was now crashing on my sister's couch. She had taken mercy on me, during one of the few times I probably didn't deserve it.

I would be out all hours of the night, sometimes days on end slinging and doing mountains of meth, only returning when I had come down enough to pass off as sober. I'd sleep for days, shower, then be back to the streets, one goal in mind.

Get loaded.

Of course, I lied to myself saying I was making money, but I smoked more than I sold. The parolee I was dating decided to steal almost four grand from me on a camping trip, so I was $3,500 broker and had already run through the majority of the settlement money, as well as the ounce of meth I had bought just a week earlier.

Sure money came and went from sales, but not enough to cover the cost. As it turns out, I was a terrible drug dealer.

A real Phony Montana, if you will.

I frequently sold at Craig's house. You know, the glass in Tim's face guy? That should give you some idea of the shady characters I was involved with, and he wasn't even the worst one. Meth does crazy shit to people. I'd watched as it turned people into living breathing demons and I was just cocky enough to stay walking among them. I didn't have a shady bone in my body, yet another square peg, round hole situation. And, while I knew everyone in the small town from my childhood, I had been in and out of lockup so much that nobody had any real loyalty to me.

I didn't know that yet, but on this particularly fucked up day—I would surely find out.

"Pass me the scale."

Craig reached over the arm of the chair and grabbed the small black scale from among the empty cigarette packs and losing scratch-offs on the cluttered nightstand, placing it in my reaching palm. I nodded my head to the sound of a System of a Down track that bled in from the living room as I weighed out a gram for a young man who definitely didn't need any more meth. Had it not been for the music, I'm almost sure you'd have been able to hear the incessant grinding of his teeth.

Craig was singing along poorly, but I didn't mind.

Actually, it was the other way around. *Not* singing along to Chop Suey was vehement blasphemy, as far as I was concerned. I'd have joined in had I not been hyper-focused on the tiny numbers being displayed on the too-small, blue rectangle at the top of the scale.

My customer sat across from me, engaging in a conscious effort to keep his limbs still.

His eyes and cheeks were sunken in and he was missing his two lower middle teeth. His clothes, though I'm sure at one time fit him perfectly, hung off of him. Like a burlap sack, draped over a skeleton.

A bag of bones.

Poor guy. He couldn't have been older than thirty but looked like a tale from the crypt, the lines of a hard life etched deep into his brow. An all too typical aesthetic around these parts. My wandering eyes pointed down at feet that were tapping furiously, in anticipation. His shoes were stained red from traipsing through red clay, hence the name of the town. Shit got everywhere. Nobody wore white shoes in Red Bluff.

I brushed the few tiny speckles of leftover shard off of the scale, closed the baggy and said, "Cash."

He handed me a crumpled hundred dollar bill, that I held up to the light, verifying its authenticity, before relinquishing the chemical gold.

"You got a pipe?" he asked expectantly, his fingers tapping the bag in a jerky rhythm.

"Nope," Craig answered for me. "We're about to leave, so you ain't gotta go home, but you can't stay here."

Craig was funny like that. We weren't leaving but for some particular reason, he wanted this guy out of his hair. Typically, he'd have let him chill so Craig could smoke up all of his dope for free, but at the moment, he was on another vibe.

The tweaker threw up a peace sign and made his way to the exit.

The house was full of dope fiends, as it always was, but tonight there were a few more than usual. I knew most of them from my elementary days, but drugs had turned them into people I didn't recognize anymore. I leaned back and sat deeper into the couch in the back room when my "ex-boyfriend" (if you could even call him that) Michael walked in with a beefy, scowling woman, just steps behind him.

"What the fuck are you doing here?" I inquired through a sneer.

"Last time I checked, this was America, Katie. I can do whatever the fuck I want," he replied, plopping onto the couch across from where I was sitting. His beady eyes shot around the room, then fell back to me. I could almost feel his gaze burning through my flesh. Heat swelled within my core, in a way only he could inspire. As far as I was concerned, he didn't deserve to look at me. It made my skin crawl that he had seen all of me. Had all of me. I was counting every second of the seven years until I would turn over all of my physical cells, and have new skin.

Skin not touched by him.

I looked over at Craig with a facial expression that read, *What the fuck?*

His reply came as expected.

"I'm not in this." Craig lifted his hands in surrender, shook his head and lifted his tweaky, wiry frame up to a standing position and made his way into the living room.

Something was up.

The strange woman had joined Michael on the nod couch. A cheap futon with tens of cigarette burns. Michael had been out of his mind lately and I instantly got the feeling that he brought the chick to fight me.

I was right.

He used to be a decent guy but, well … *drugs.*

I pulled a knife from each pocket and set them on my lap. More of an intimidation factor than anything. I didn't think I'd actually have to use them, but—you never knew. I lit a cigarette and took a long inhale before setting it in the ashtray to free my hands to get high.

I wasn't afraid of the girl. Growing up in gladiator school made me a pretty tough broad and though she was big, I was bigger. Even underweight from extreme drug use, I was five feet ten and my fists were heavy as any man. She gave me the typical once-over. Never having met me, I assume she expected me to look somewhat different. I had a reputation about me, one that would make any sane, rational person think twice than to cross me. We weren't dealing with sane, rational people.

I kept hearing the squeak and click of the front door opening and closing from the living room not twenty-five feet away. Quickly, I was overwhelmed by a sinking feeling in my stomach.

Something is off.

I tried to ignore the pestering intuition—had I been sober, I would've taken heed at the first twinge; my gut never told a lie. On second thought, had I been sober, I wouldn't have been there at all. I shrugged it off and began twisting the glass pressed to my dry, cracked lips and exhaled. Smoke billowed directly into the girl's face, which she waved away, revealing what I believed to be her signature look. An irritated scowl.

"What's up. You here for me?" I said through a coy grin. The words exited my mouth, the tail end taking shape as a haughty laugh. To me, her presence was comical.

She wasn't laughing.

I held the pipe in the air between us as a peace offering.

"We could be friends instead, if you want. You might've not gotten the full story." I said the words knowing the translation would be received.

You might want to rethink your intent. I make a better friend than an enemy.

"I don't want shit from you," she growled.

I smiled and let out a quiet chuckle, before my ears perked once again. More doors opening and shutting. A wave of anxiety rushed over me and a tremor ran down my leg, settling into my nervous feet.

I couldn't ignore it this time.

I quietly lifted myself off of the couch, tiptoed to the door and peeked my head around the corner, only to see upward of ten men sitting in the living room. One of them … was Bullet. I shuddered at the realization. My mouth went dry and an internal alarm rang loud with warning of imminent danger.

He had just gotten out of prison for some pretty heinous shit. I didn't know the exact charges, as everything you heard about people in this town was a game of telephone, filtered through highly addictive substances, but I knew when he showed up—somebody was getting robbed.

It was a setup. They were going to try to rob me.

I looked at the two knives in my hand and quickly assessed. I couldn't brandish both and get my things together at the same time. I opted for the sharper, serrated piece and slipped the other in my pocket, slowly backing into the room.

It was too late. They were made, and they knew it.

A man I had never seen before barreled in as I was gathering my belongings from the couch. His eyes bulged from their sunken sockets, as his psychotic voice thundered through the room, with a confidence only being up for a week straight can give you.

"Give me your dope!"

My nostrils flared as a scowl curled my brow and I spat out my favorite words.

"Fuck you!"

He clocked me. Hard.

Like a deep breath, I expanded. My soul stood beside me as I watched the event play out like a scene in a movie. Rocked by the blow, I swayed—but my knees held firm. The next moments occurred in segments, as if someone was changing the channel on each frame. The flashes moved forward in sequence and slowly around me, my vision cutting in and out.

My arm swept the nightstand, clearing the surface of its pile of clutter. Click. Slashing, slashing like a madwoman. Click. I fell into the couch with my back against the wall, as he struggled to find an angle where he wasn't exposed. Click.

A voice I didn't recognize as my own escaped from my quivering lips.

"Back the fuck up or I'll gut you like a fucking fish!"

End scene. I could barely breathe. A line of strange and familiar faces lined the frame of the door, each with eyes of different width but the same shock. The widest of eyes belonged to Craig.

"CRAIG!" The words felt foreign in the moment, as if I'd forgotten how to speak. "WHAT THE FUCK, CRAIG!"

Craig took a timid step into the room, eyes darting, his meth poisoned mind trying to process the situation in real time. He grasped at the back of his head with shaky palms and shouted back at me, bold lies dripping through his teeth.

"I DIDN'T FUCKING KNOW! WHAT THE FUCK IS HAPPENING?"

I didn't believe him. Things just didn't go as planned, and someone was going to die in his house if he didn't do something, and fast.

"BACK THE FUCK UP!" I screamed at the foreign man. He did.

"THIS IS YOUR FUCKING HOUSE, CRAIG. NOTHING HAPPENS WITHOUT YOUR PERMISSION!" I tried to still my shaky voice but it wavered nonetheless. My fight or flight was in full gear. I would've given anything in that moment to flight, but I was backed into a corner. Luckily, I had the fight of a rabid dog in savage self-preservation.

"SHE WALKS OUT OF HERE, GUYS! JUST GET YOUR SHIT— AND LEAVE!"

I gulped in air as if I had been held underwater and my eyes shot around the room, assessing my optimal route of escape. My back pressed firmly against the wall gave me full visibility of my assailant, as he hovered over me in an embarrassed rage.

Always keep your back to the wall so they can't rush you from behind.

"Him first. He's not coming behind me." The phrase dripped from my tight mouth, slow and foul, like poisoned honey, as I gestured toward the strong left hook that was fuming just out of arms reach. My jaw was hot and I could tell it was beginning to swell.

"JOSH! GET THE FUCK OUT OF THE ROOM!" Craig commanded, pointing to the exit.

Josh gave me one last look of pure hate before he staggered in defeat toward the door, spewing, "This isn't fucking over," as he exited stage left. I took a deep breath and stood up on my Gumby-like legs. I was sure there were bones in there somewhere, but they felt like goo. Each step I took in faith, not feeling my feet on the floor beneath me.

Keep it together, Kate. You're almost out. Show no fear. You got this. Stand tall.

My own voice echoed between my ears. I was almost out of dodge. Just a few more steps and I would be safe. I just had to make it through the living room and out the door.

Simple enough, right? Wrong.

The thought of closing the short distance to the front door felt like I was preparing to swim a mile, through a piranha-filled river. I gathered my wits and observed my belongings that were strewn about the room. It wasn't worth the risk to collect them.

"NO FUCK THAT!" a deep, raspy voice boomed from the living room and echoed down the hall, sending a chill down my spine. It was Bullet. Hungry for dope and out for blood. Even Craig wouldn't want to come up against Bullet, his house or not. He met me at the door, with a gleaming straight razor in his hand.

Bullet could only be described as a junkie madman. Jackal eyes and a jumbled mess of decaying teeth behind thin white lips. Masses of penitentiary muscle still hung heavy on his frame. A wife-beater—soaked in sweat—revealing the racist prison tats that covered his freckled Irish skin.

I don't know that any of them were *actually* racist. I looked at it as something they picked up in a book called *How to Prison: A Survival Guide*. You end up in prison, you go with your race or you die. That's just how it was. Years of conditioning, with no real merit.

However, the fact that I didn't share their belief system didn't sit right with them.

I was white as snow.

Purebred.

Frequently, they would hurl choice slurs in my direction with the word "lover" after them—to which I'd agree antagonistically, infuriating them more. I was a human lover. The foster-mothers who raised and loved me were of all different races. You don't just *casually forget* that because some dumb fuck, who couldn't pass a fifth-grade math test, has something to say about it.

I quickly assessed the distance between him and the door. It was too far. If I turned my back now, I had no way of defending myself. We were in a standoff.

Each second felt like minutes and I wondered why he hadn't rushed me yet. Something must've shaken him though he appeared as normal as ever. Normal meaning insane.

"Give me your fucking dope, you cunt, or you won't live to tell this fucking tale, you dirty bitch!"

Spit flew from his lips as he sputtered the cold words of warning.

"You'll get my dope when you pry it from my cold dead fingers, punk!"

I matched his twisted energy effortlessly.

Who just said that? The words came from my lips but I didn't call them forth. A murderous chill ran through my veins. I had never known whether or not I was capable of murder until this moment. I wasn't a confrontational person. But let me tell you, the sheer instinct of survival triggered by someone trying to take your life will bring out the assassin in you. It's genetic. It's been woven into our code. My life was at risk and if it was you or me, as it turns out, I was pretty OK with the dead person being you. Maybe it was the look of pure insanity in my eyes that saved my life that night.

"You're lucky I don't throw it straight across your neck!" His attempt at intimidation fell flat and I could sense his growing frustration. Bullet wasn't one that typically lost these types of battles. Especially against a girl.

I, on the other hand, felt as though I had activated some form of ancient Goth warrior blood that had been lying dormant in my veins or something, because again, my reply shocked even me.

"You can try, but if you miss you're weaponless, so you might want to think that one through."

The words of war sat above the quiet shock that had settled within the walls of the house, like oil to water. Ten people sat observing the insanity and not one made so much as a peep.

I wasn't backing down an inch and it infuriated him. His face shook as he silently raged, veins bulging from his neck and forehead. The tweaky cowards in the living room hovered, thirsty like a starving pack of hyenas. One moment of weakness. One second of fear—they would pounce.

I showed none.

If I was going to die tonight, I wasn't going to be the only one. One minute I was counting the ways I would destroy anyone who meant to do me harm, and the next—it was over.

"PUT THE FUCKING KNIVES DOWN! KATIE—GO! NO ONE FOLLOWS HER!" Shock clothed my face as Craig put himself between Bullet and me, giving me enough space to walk out the door. You didn't have to tell me twice. I kept my eyes locked on Bullet, as I put distance between us, each step heavy, holding the weight of my entire existence. I scanned the room from left to right, the blade following my gaze as I walked backward, clumsily to the door. I swung it open in disbelief. I could still hear the sound of the door slamming into the frame behind me when my mind said: *Run!*

I booked it.

I'd never run so fast in my life. I had it in my mind that they would try to chase me. If they caught me, I wouldn't be so lucky this time. I ran full speed down Walnut Street, toward the safety of my sister Niki's apartment. Suddenly, a yellow pickup truck screeched to a halt and a stranger's screams filled the night.

"Are you OK?! I swear I had nothing to do with it! I'll take you wherever you need to go!"

My reaction was primal. Like an ally cat mistaken for prey. My eyes gleamed and darted, my hair stood up on end as I curled my back in recoil. The man was frantic and seemed sincere but I didn't know him and I didn't trust anyone at this point. People I had known since childhood just witnessed the attempt of me being robbed and murdered. At best, they did nothing to stop it and at worst—they were in on it. I screamed through the night so loudly it could've curdled blood.

"GETTT—THE FUUCKKK—AWWWAYY FROMM MEEEEEE!"

His tires squealed, as he punched a lead foot to the gas. One minute he was in vision and the next he was gone. Leaving only a cloud of dark smoke as proof he had been there at all. I continued to run until I reached my sister's street.

I couldn't walk into her house looking like this. Mascara tears streamed down my face as I failed to hold back my sobs. It was ten o'clock. She would be asleep soon and once she was, I would sneak in, but for now, I would sit on the curb. And cry.

Chest heaving, trouble breathing, choking, coughing, bawled.

I cried.

* * *

SCOTTSDALE WAY, RED BLUFF, CA, MAY 7TH 2008.

"Katie ..."

I could hear a voice in my dream that sounded all too familiar. It swirled around in pieces, a ghost haunting my subconscious. The voice faded off, before ringing through my dream again.

"*Katie!*"

It was my sister. In the waking world. She had come home to eat lunch on her break from her job at the local Walmart. I don't know how long I had been asleep at that point, but I woke up to her standing, arms crossed, at the foot of the couch I was sprawled across. Her big, beautiful, morning-glory blue eyes gleamed at me and her perfect brows furrowed in a look of desperate concern as she shook her head gently.

"You just gonna sleep for a week?"

"Sorry, sis, I'm just really tired ... I haven't been feeling really good."

That was all true. I was coming down, so I was exhausted. I was also not feeling good. But not because I had the flu. I was in full-blown withdrawal.

Withdrawal from meth sucks, but it was light in comparison to other drugs. You just slept for days, then woke up so hungry that you ate the entire house. The emotional symptoms were worse, but I wasn't there yet.

"You know ... I'd really like to believe you, but something's up. It makes me sick to my stomach and I don't know what to do. I've tried to look the other way because I know you've gotten a pretty shit hand, but you gotta do something—*anything*—other than live on my couch."

"I'm working on it," I said, wiping the sleep from my eyes, not fully in this reality yet. This was not the way I wanted to wake up—today or ever. She was right, of course, but I didn't know what the fuck I was supposed to do. Nobody gave me a manual for how to adult and I wasn't even close to figuring it out. As a matter of fact, it seemed I did all of the things wrong quite naturally.

Fucking up was my gift.

"What?" she inquired with an air of valid irritation. "Working on what? Because you can't work on shit when you're passed out for five days straight, Kate."

"Job Corps—I called a lady—I'm supposed to have an interview on Tuesday."

Job Corps was the poor man's military. It was a shit option, but they gave you housing and job training and now that I was broke and knew I couldn't trust a soul in this town, I was desperate. It was the only plan I could think of.

A look of subtle surprise graced her beautiful face.

Niki wasn't just pretty. She was gorgeous. Long, flowing, dark locks that swung around her narrow waistline. Huge, deep, ocean eyes and a smile that could make any red-blooded male's pressure rise with a single flash.

"Wow—OK. That could be really good for you." Her cautious optimism caught me off guard. Mainly because I'd said I was going to do a bunch of things and did approximately none of them. I scooted up into a sitting position to make room for her to sit at my feet.

"You know I love you, Kate—I just don't know what to do. I don't want to put you out but I feel like I'm enabling you."

She might have been. If she was, it was the first time anyone had "enabled" me in my life, so all I saw was, for once, someone actually gave enough fucks *about* me to see past the fucked up *in* me.

Somebody to make sure I had a safe place to lay my head, even if it seemed like I didn't deserve it.

"I have to think about my kids, Kate."

Her kids were safe. I never let anyone see where I lived and nobody ever had my phone number at Niki's anyways, but I got it. Loving me was a risk some people couldn't take.

"I get it, Nik … I told you I called the Job Corps lady. She's coming to interview me on Tuesday."

It was Friday.

"Where's the interview?" Niki inquired with a hint of suspicion.

"At McDonald's," I replied through the yawn that was stretching my face wide. "Ah … on Antelope. She said she'd meet me at McDonald's, on Antelope. Tuesday, at two o'clock."

I was hoping that was all the information she'd need because that was all the information I had.

It seemed to satisfy her.

"You need a shower," she said, rising to her feet. "And clean up the kitchen please. I get off in a few hours and I don't want the boys seeing their aunt passed out again when I bring them home from day care or we're gonna have a problem. Get up. Take care of your shit. Capisce?"

"I'm up … I got it. Have a good day; I'll see you when you get home."

Niki grabbed her keys and took one last glance in my direction with her eyebrows raised, as a punctuation mark on her previous instructions.

"I got it, Niki."

"OK," she replied as she stepped out into the sunlight and shut the door behind her.

Fuck, I thought to myself. How the fuck was I going to stay awake?

Coffee. Sunlight. Shower. Do things. Move. I stood up and walked toward the bay window and opened the blinds. The sun poured in, nearly blinding me.

"Ah … fuck!" I closed my eyes as a knee-jerk reaction to the sudden influx of brightness, letting my eyes adjust. I opened one eye, blinked and then opened both. It was going to be a long day.

I stumbled into the kitchen to the coffee pot that was half full and ice cold. I poured a large cup and put it in the microwave hastily, splashing the black liquid onto the dirty plate below. Every beep of a button sounded like a scream. I waited, slumped over on the counter, for the minute to expire, watching every second count down until it the tiny screen read one second. I snatched the door open just in time, beating the final beep of completion that might've sent me over the edge.

I stood in the kitchen and chugged the too-hot-to-gulp coffee—burning my mouth and throat as I ingested the much-needed caffeine. I didn't care. I just needed to wake up. I couldn't handle a fight with Niki about the dirty kitchen or my inability to be conscious when she got back.

Nothing. Coffee is worthless when you're coming down from meth.

I found my way to the shower and sat on the floor of the tub, washing my hair and body, too exhausted to stand. The hot water rained down on my swollen face. I could hide the yellowing of the fading bruise on my jawline with makeup, but it was still tender to the touch.

Every movement took more energy than I had, but I had to try.

I pulled myself up off the floor, rummaged around for some clean clothes and avoided any and all mirrors as I made my way down the stairs to the living room again. What I would have given to fall onto the couch and never get up again.

It beckoned me, looking like a haven I had been locked out of.

Sit, I told myself. Sitting wouldn't completely prevent me from passing out, but lying down would ensure it. Sitting was the only viable option.

The thought of cleaning the kitchen was the mental equivalent of climbing Mount Everest.

Every iota of energy I'd had had been depleted from the shower and I'd need to build up my reserves again before I could make an attempt. The only place that was uncomfortable enough that I might be forced to stay conscious was the computer chair. I sat down and turned on the desktop, made my way onto the web browser and opened up Myspace, praying it would hold my attention.

"Down with the Sickness" blared from the speakers as I opened my page.

"*Whoa!*" I yelled in alarm as my hand darted to the volume knob at the bottom of the white tower and spun it to zero, the aftershock still ringing through my ears.

That should wake me up.

I had a message. I opened it and quickly saw it was from Allie. *What the fuck does she want?*

Allie had been a close friend when I was living in a juvenile parole home in Paradise before my last violation and our friendship had not ended on the best of terms. Long story short, she thought I was trying to get with her ex-boyfriend. I wasn't. She was a pretty insecure girl and while I tried to let it slide, she wanted to fight me. A good old hick town rough and tumble. Didn't work out so well for her. My last memory of her was me savagely straddling her in a park as my crushing fists fell down on her in rapid repetition when a Good Samaritan ran up and said—

"BREAK IT UP; I ALREADY CALLED THE COPS!"

Cops just so happens to be my safe word.

I could be having a psychotic break and if I hear the word cop, I snap back into reality like a light switch being turned on and make a break for.

Imagine my surprise when I found that this Myspace message was a peace offering. She had moved to LA and her boyfriend's best friend was being signed to a record label. Somehow she had convinced him to feature me on his album. *What a crock of shit.*

I didn't trust her as far as I could throw her, which I summed up pretty directly in my reply. I spent the next hour sending messages back and forth with Allie—each message from her painting a more convincing picture. I looked at the clock. *Fuck! The kitchen. I had to clean the kitchen.* Niki would be home any minute.

I sprung up from the chair, ran to the kitchen and frantically started doing dishes and tossing trash from the counters into the overflowing bin. I heard a car pull into the driveway. *Fuck.* I couldn't look to see if it was her. I would lose time.

I scrubbed down the counters the best I could before shoving the trash down to a closable level and grabbing the broom. The door swung open just as I was sweeping the last bit of the pile into the dustpan. My nephews ran in with a burst of energy, throwing their backpacks on the floor by the door and bolted into the newly cleaned kitchen for a snack.

"AUNT KATIE, CAN WE PLAY HIDE AND SEEK!"

My nephew Tate's little arms wrapped themselves around my leg as he shook me expectantly.

"Maybe in a bit, my love. I'm just finishing up the kitchen."

Jay had already climbed up on the counter to search the cupboard for a snack.

"Hey! Get down! What do you want? I'll get it."

"Fruit snacks," Jay replied, slowly climbing down off the counter.

"Yeah! Fruit snacks!" Tate mimicked, in an excited singsong, as Niki rounded the corner of the open door with bags of groceries in her hand. The water was still running from the dishes and it was pretty obvious I had just finished cleaning.

"In the nick of time, huh?" she said as she flashed a grin, pleased that I had followed her instructions.

"You know me," I replied in relief.

She was smiling. I liked when she smiled. Especially at me, because it definitely wasn't the typical facial expression I got from people these days. But I'd forget about that in this moment. For only a moment.

"Help me with the groceries," she said, lugging the bags onto the still wet counters.

"Catch!" I said as I passed off the fruit snacks to the nephews in a single toss. Jay caught his, while Tate's smacked him right in the face.

"Awe, man!" he said as he scooped up the colorful package from the floor.

Niki had already begun putting groceries away like the machine she was. I joined her in silence.

How was I going to tell her? How would she react?

I had to tell her something. I assumed she'd think it was a terrible idea. Most of my ideas seemed to be terrible to my biological family. But it was an option. A better option than Job Corps, at least in my mind. I could escape this town and have an opportunity I would never have gotten otherwise.

I placed the new cereal alongside the boxes of opened ones in the cupboard next to the refrigerator before turning to grab the few cans of chili left in the bag. They were already in Niki's hand. She just stood there, looking at me and holding the cans, displaying no effort to pass them to me or put them away. Just holding them, staring, with her head slightly cocked. I could always tell when her brain was working overtime because a very specific look would cross her face. She bit the side of her cheek and her perfect eyebrows arched, creating a squint in her eyes.

She nodded upward.

"What's up with you?"

She knew.

She didn't know what she knew, but she knew something. All of us sisters could read each other like a book. My eyes darted away from her in hesitation.

"Mm-hmm. Something's up ... is it the Job Corps thing?"

I leaned back on the counter, folded my arms in front of my substantial breast and took a deep inhale.

"Kinda."

"What, you're not gonna go?" Disappointment began to make its way across her pretty face. I hated that look. Go back to the smile, I thought to myself. I like that face better.

"Well ..." I hesitated again. "It's one of the options."

She looked puzzled.

"*One* of the options?"

"Yeah—*one* of the options," I replied, grabbing the chili from her and turning to place it in the pantry.

"What's the other option?" Niki opened the fridge and reached for a Coors Light, popping the tab open, obviously thinking it necessary for what I was about to say next.

She took a swig.

"Well, my old friend from Paradise sent me a message on Myspace and said I could come stay with her. Her boyfriend's best friend is getting a record deal and he wants me to be on the album ..."

Niki took another drink of her beer as I twisted my hands around each other, anxiously awaiting her response.

"A record deal in Paradise?" she inquired in disbelief.

"No," I said, attempting to hide my irritation, "she's in LA now. Allie—you remember me talking about her."

"The girl you beat up?" she said in a half-laugh, half-stunned response.

"This is why I didn't want to tell you ..."

"Kate, it just doesn't seem like she's that good of a friend. You're just gonna whisk yourself off to a big dangerous city where you have nobody but someone you haven't seen since you fought them? Sorry, but it just doesn't sound like the best plan." She took another gulp of her beer. "If you ask me."

"I didn't."

"What?"

"I didn't ask you. I *told* you. I *told* you it was one of the options. I'm an adult. I'm not asking for permission to live *my* life. Job Corps seems like another prison. I've done my time and this could be a beautiful opportunity for me and you're shitting all over it."

"I just—"

"*Not* to mention, the situation you described is much like I have here so—what do I have to lose?"

She recoiled at the sting of my words. It was true though. It wasn't my intention to hurt her, but the facts remained the facts. She let me stay with her partially out of obligation and partially out of pity. All of it was wrapped in love, but we didn't really grow up together, so our relationship was more of cousins than of sisters. She cared about me, there was no question. But, we were all healing from our own versions of hell and sometimes it was hard to see outside ourselves. She had made it pretty clear that the days of me sleeping on her couch were coming to an end and I didn't blame her. But, the fact remained that the situation I had in Red Bluff was no better, if not exactly the same as what she saw Los Angeles being for me in her mind.

The only difference was I knew what happened if I stayed here. I'd continue getting loaded and either end up incarcerated again or worse—dead.

That could potentially happen in LA too, but at least it was a chance at a new life, something I so desperately wanted.

Did I trust Allie? No.

Allie was selfish, insecure and not a generally good person. But, she was going to buy me a bus ticket and get me the fuck out of this "Shit Town, America," and that was good enough for me.

"Are you gonna tell Mom? Or Jamie?"

"Why? So they can say the same shit you just said but not give me another option?"

"Job—"

"I'm *not* going to Job Corps, Niki."

"But you said it was one of—"

"Not—anymore!"

Niki shook her head before saying the words out of anger that would ring in my ears for the next six months.

"Well, when you fall flat on your face, you're not coming back here."

Chapter Six

UNION STATION, LOS ANGELES, CA, MAY 8TH 2008.

I opened my eyes to a strange figure standing above me. I had curled up on a bench at Union Station as soon as my bus had arrived at eight o'clock that morning. More than two hours had passed since I had texted Allie that I had arrived. I don't know if you've ever tried sleeping on a Greyhound bus before, but if you haven't—the emphasis is on the word *tried*. Vain attempts left my limbs cramped and kinked and I was weary with exhaustion. However, I was so tired I could've slept for hours on that cold hard bench had a shadow not triggered my internal alarm, jolting me awake. It was Allie, though she looked far different from the country girl I had once known. The city had painted her with long acrylic nails, brightly colored clothing and oversized jewelry. My groggy eyes made their way down her frame, to her chubby feet, shoved into too-small silver stilettos. Spilling through the straps, resembling sausages about to burst from their casings. How did she even get them on? I wondered to myself.

"You made it!" she exclaimed in a shrill high pitch, sending a shock wave through my not yet fully awakened brain.

"I did," I half mumbled, wiping phantom mascara from under my eyes.

I sat up, stretched and looked around for my bags, expecting them to be stolen. They weren't. Maybe my luck was starting to turn around.

"Is this your stuff?" she asked, popping her gum and beginning the flagrant assault of verbs and nouns that filled my ears at an unprecedented rate. Blah, blah, blah. I cut her off.

"I need to get some food." You could say I was dry, but I was tired and hungry. It was dry or mean, and dry seemed the best option of the two.

"Oh, for sure … Mik is with us so we'll drop him off and then we'll get something to eat."

"Mik's the rapper?"

"Yeah … he and I kinda had a thing—like we're probably in love with each other but it is what it is …" She continued to speak rapidly as I shook my head, trying to digest the onslaught of volume that flooded the air from her tiny mouth. How could so much information come so fast? She rattled on about their affair as I nodded with a cocked brow, attempting to hide my annoyance. After rambling for another forty-five seconds, she ended the monologue with "Don't tell Keith."

"And Keith is?"

"My boyfriend," she said with her eyebrows raised to an unspeakable height. "You'll see."

I definitely would. We approached a silver Impala with two men sitting inside. Keith was handsome, a Cupid's bow sitting atop his full mouth, a fitted LA cap hiding his brow. His hair fell past his shoulders and his big brown eyes didn't glance my way once. I observed a white Pro-Club T-shirt only complemented by a humble gold chain and jeans, nothing too flashy. There was something about him. Something I couldn't place.

Mik was dressed similarly, though his energy spoke volumes without him having said a word.

Allie helped me put my suitcase in the trunk before we slid into the low backseat.

Mik acknowledged me with a wave and a grin and Keith stared straight ahead. He was quiet but it wasn't alarming. My daily word count tolerance had surely already been reached, so silence was hardly an issue for me.

As he pulled into the heavy traffic of downtown Los Angeles, rap music came over the speakers and everyone started nodding their head to the beat. It was an artist I had never heard before but it was good. Great actually.

"Who is this?" I asked Allie just loud enough for her to hear me over the blaring speakers.

"It's Mik!" she said excitedly, pointing to the gentleman in the passenger seat. "He's the one I was telling you about!" She continued to nod her head and rap along to every word as if she were starring in a music video. Mik glanced back with a look of pride before facing front again.

I was in shock.

This is actually happening? This is the best day of my life!

The "best day of my life" was a lie wrapped in a pretty bow, but for a moment—if only for a moment—I thought all of my dreams were coming true.

We pulled up outside of an apartment complex on the corner of La Brea and Slauson. There were bars on the windows like I had only seen in the movies. I was in Inglewood. A city notoriously known for gangs and drugs. I had heard it referenced in rap songs but never thought I'd actually be there.

"Don't be scared! That's normal in LA!" Allie tried to soothe my nonexistent anxious thoughts. I laughed.

"I'm not scared of bars that keep people from getting in. I'm scared of the bars that keep people from getting out," I replied with a quip, resting my tired head on the window.

Mik and Keith got out of the car, the engine still running.

"Be right back," Keith yelled through the open driver door window after shutting it with care. I looked at Allie.

"We're not staying here?"

"Oh no … like we kinda live here … I mean … I pay the rent but … we're gonna stay at another place where I can work."

"Oh OK," I said, not thinking much of it. I didn't have the energy to think. "What did you say you did again?"

"I give massages!" she replied.

I watched her apply lip gloss in a small Maybelline compact that she snapped shut after pursing her lips then redirecting her focus to me. The pieces weren't clicking together yet, but my little brain was lighting up in places I knew all too well.

Something wasn't right; I just didn't know what.

Just then Allie popped open the door to get in the front seat.

"I could do that," I thought out loud. "Do you make good money? Did you have to go to school?"

"Oh! You could totally do it! No, silly, you just put an ad online … I made eight hundred dollars yesterday."

Seemed like a lot for massages. The pieces. Still not clicking.

"Sometimes I sleep with them, but not all the time."

Click. She was a prostitute. I swallowed the information slowly, digesting each facet individually, but held no judgment. She was a grown woman and could do whatever she wanted. I went to ask more questions, but right as

I did, Keith came through the gate of the building and hopped in the car. For some reason I wasn't comfortable talking openly around him. Maybe because she wasn't.

We drove. We drove and we drove. I had never seen so many buildings next to each other. City after city, from edge to edge. Where I come from, you drove through a town, then there was at least twenty miles of dead nowhere before you got to the next small town. Not here. They just kept going. We inched along in the mess of traffic for hours to travel not more than ten miles.

Talk about culture shock.

The constant influx of words from Allie's mouth to my ears was exhausting. Cracking offbeat jokes, trying to make me laugh. It took the edge off but I was still filled with anxiety, trying to figure out the whole scope of the situation I was in, but I was tired and seemed to be safe for the time being. I rested my head on the window again, taking it all in. The car went quiet for a moment and I thought I might fall asleep.

No luck.

"Hey, Kay …" My lids fluttered open and I looked toward the source of the voice. It was Allie.

"*SURPRISE!*" In a quick moment, Allie ripped a wig off of her shaved head and burst out in maniacal laughter. I thought she had lost her mind. It was in that moment I contemplated whether or not I had made a serious lapse in judgment.

"*IT'S A WIG!*" she exclaimed.

"I see that," was my stunned reply. "What—*the fuck*—happened to your hair?!"

I gripped my own waist-length, chestnut locks, in fear that the man sitting next to her was the villain. Who in their right mind would shave their own head?

"My ex shaved it because I left him." She offered the information shamelessly, as if it were shop talk.

What. The. Fuck.

"It's cool though cuz now I don't have to spend hours doing my hair! I just pop on a wig and—*voila!* You didn't even know, huh!"

No. *I didn't.*

I wished I still didn't.

"You crazy, girl." Keith uttered his second sentence in the now four hours I had known him. He didn't talk much. Almost like he had a secret to keep—because he did. One that I'd find out soon enough.

"Papa—I wanna stop and get us something to eat … Here—*HERE!*" She pointed at an El Pollo Loco frantically. The nickname—*Papa*—sent another weird vibe through my filter but paled in comparison to the other oddities of the hour, so I didn't think much else about it. In hindsight, there were so many signs, I would spend countless hours in the future wondering how I had missed them. Was it because I was young? Naive? I trusted people I shouldn't, assuming they were like me. *Surely not all people are horrible; I should give this one a chance.* But, thinking other people had the same heart as me typically led mine to being broken.

He pulled into the fast-food chicken chain and parked in the lot.

"Money, please …" she voiced her polite demand, to which he placed two twenty-dollar bills from the large wad he had pulled from his pocket in her extended palm. *Why was he giving her money? I thought she made eight hundred dollars yesterday?* I shook the suspicion from my mind yet again.

"Come on!" she waved me out of the car.

I was in some sort of twilight episode it seemed. He would wait in the car for us as we went inside to get our order to go. I gathered that she liked to get me away from him, so she could talk to me without prying ears. She ordered for the both of them then looked at me expectantly.

"Um … what's good here?"

The menu was foreign. I had never seen an El Pollo Loco before.

"Bitch. Everything."

"Umm, OK … I'll just have what you got." I didn't fucking care. I was starving and salivating like one of Pavlov's dogs. Plus, there were more people in that one El Pollo Loco than typically frequented the local Walmart in my hometown, and it made me nervous. I had never seen so many people. Swarming and swirling and then buzzing out the door to carry on about their day. We were waiting for the order at the end of the pickup counter when she grabbed my arm and began offering more unwanted dialogue.

"So like—I make the money and he keeps it but—I always keep the change."

What the fuck again. Why did I get the feeling that she was bread-crumbing me for a bigger plot twist later? This was all useless information, but when you put it all together it seemed like she was trying to hint in the direction of disclosure. I didn't get it. Never in my life would I have assumed she was capable of what she was doing. Still, I grew uncomfortable and stumbled over my response.

"Uhhh—yeah—I mean—Honestly, it's none of my business …"

Before she could respond, a voice rang through the air.

"Order number 48!"

Just in the nick of time.

* * *

BEST WESTERN INN & SUITES, REDONDO BEACH, CA, MAY 8TH 2008.

After what seemed like an eternity spent in stop-and-go traffic, we pulled into the huge parking lot of a Best Western hotel. The signature palm trees of Los Angeles lined the streets and I could smell salt water in the air. The ocean was nearby. We pulled into a covered parking space and everyone hopped out. Keith grabbed my luggage from the trunk as I stood dazed, looking around at the huge hotel. The city buzzed and sung with movement as, what seemed like, hundreds of cars whirred by. It was at that moment that it hit me.

I was in LA. I was here. I—had arrived.

We climbed the stairs to the room in silence and Keith popped open the door with the swipe of a key card.

"Where are we?" I asked in wonder, looking around at the palm tree silhouettes framing the cloudless sky. "LA still?"

"Technically, we're in the South Bay—Redondo Beach."

"Rhododendron Beach?" I struggled to remember the simple words.

"Re-don-do. Redondo Beach."

I had never been to a town with *beach* in the name before, so in my mind this was some sort of upscale land.

"You want to take a shower?" Allie asked, walking to the bathroom and popping open the door.

"Umm … yeah—probably need one," I said with an exhausted laugh.

"Cool! I'll take one with you. It'll save time."

Time? What time were we saving?

I went to ask, but before I could, she grabbed me by my oversized jacket and pulled me into the tiny, off-white bathroom, following closely behind.

"We're gonna take a shower, Papa!" she yelled through the small crack of the closing door before it clicked behind her. She pushed in the button lock with a click and turned on the shower. I looked at her confused. Not that we hadn't gotten ready together before. Most of our friendship was spent partying in Chico, a notorious college town. We had a vast amount of memories, getting ready to go out to the house and dorm parties, but everything she had done, since me getting in the Impala at Union Station, had reeked of odd, strange behavior that she passed off as normal. I expected her to start undressing but paused to observe before making any moves myself. She pulled a glass meth pipe out of the inside pocket of her tiny jean jacket.

Ah. Yeah. That makes sense.

"You smoke?" she asked, raising the pipe to her lips and putting a flame to it before I could even answer. Her intense gaze watched the ball of the pipe as it filled up with smoke and she began twirling and sucking in a jerky motion.

"I—"

I didn't know how to answer that question. Here I was thinking I was leaving my dope days behind and the first day in my new life, my drug of choice is being smoked right in front of me. As a rule I think I'm a pretty headstrong individual. Not when it came to substances though. I was hooked and staying clean when drugs aren't around you is one thing. Saying no when you are at the week mark of a treacherous comedown and dope is readily available, within arm's reach, is quite another.

She passed me the pipe. The dope was blue. I had never seen blue meth before. I looked at it from multiple angles before looking back at her.

"It's *blue?*" I stated half question, half matter of factly.

"Yeah, it's bomb. We're right near the border so we get the good shit here straight from Mexico. No cut."

I liked the sound of that. The cut in the dope in my hometown gave me sores that resembled blisters. Mostly on my fingers and they were disgusting.

Fuck it.

I lifted the pipe to my lips and began to roll it smoothly. Left. Pause. Right. Pause. *Faster.* Left. Pause. Right. Pause. *Faster.* Left right, left right. Inhaling at every turn. I had lungs of steel and could've finished the small bowl in one hit.

"Easy!" Allie said, breaking my concentration. "It's some *strong-ass shit!* Just see how it hits you before you go all Brittany Murphy in *Spun* on me!"

I exhaled as the chemicals hit my bloodstream like a freight train. This was some gourmet shit. My head buzzed and the once trickles of the shower head now sounded like a waterfall.

I was back. Vampire blood. Beam—me—up.

I could've stopped there and been spun for three days without trying but—an addict *with* dope is an addict who *does* dope. The ritual is almost as intoxicating as the actual high. The loading the pipe. Melting it down. Watching the crystals become liquid and the small waft of smoke forming before pulling it to your lips. The grace of the twirl, showing the fellow observing addict how skillfully you twist, as you suck and then finally— blowing out the cloud.

It wasn't just the getting high. It was all of it.

We passed the pipe back and forth a few times before Allie began shedding her layers, the last being the wig she placed on the back of the toilet. The small room filled with the smell of chemicals, thick haze blending with the steam of the shower. Allie looked at herself in the mirror. She was a bit dumpy with a beautiful face. Always had been. With the right clothes, she had an undeniable confidence, but when they came off, her insecurities washed over her.

"Do I look like a grandma?" Allie asked me, still observing herself in the mirror.

I looked her once over. That particular brand of thought had never crossed my mind before but now that it had made its way out of her mouth and into my ears, I could see why she would make such a comparison. Her triangular-shaped breast crossed her chest, creating a double U format and her nipples pointed to her soft and wide midsection. The place where her pelvis met her stomach inverted, leaving another double U. Both her nipples and her belly button faced the floor as if they had sunk into place.

She wasn't fat. Not by any means of the word. But the mix of her genetics, with extreme drug abuse, left her with the form resembling that of a Renaissance painting.

"No, of course not," I replied, looking away hesitantly, beginning to undress myself. "Why would you even ask that?" I'm usually a pretty blunt person, but hurting her feelings and stirring up her insecurities were not a high priority on my to-do list today. Just my existence seemed to make her unnerved enough. No need confirming on my part.

"I just—everything just faces *down,* like …" She picked up her left tit and let it drop heavily into its rightful place a few inches too low on her chest. She seemed to like playing this game of hating herself, but I refused to join in.

"You're just being hard on yourself. Stop. We all do it. We pick ourselves apart. It's not that bad, Al—"

"It's not *that* bad?!" she exclaimed, a flicker of annoyance fueled by crystal meth in her eyes.

"You know what I meant, don't start—"

I unsnapped my dirty Victoria Secret bra and let it fall to the floor. It was the only good bra I had and I wore it every day. The straps had discolored and the fabric holding the underwire was beginning to fray, creating a hole. It poked the shit out of me, but I didn't care. It was my favorite bra. I looked at myself in the mirror. I had my mother's breasts.

I had stayed a virgin until I was seventeen because I was insecure about the size of my dainty nipples. But, when I did take off my shirt in front of the first man to get that far, his facial expression told it all before words had a chance to.

You have the most perfect breasts I've ever seen in real life.

I didn't believe him. Even if they were the most perfect breasts he had seen, he surely hadn't seen many. I had an unfair advantage. I was filled with insecurities at that young of an age. I could barely take a compliment because my sisters were so beautiful and I had been told on multiple occasions that I was the "Ugly Duckling." I'm sure this statement was meant to be said in the way that the ugly duckling turns into a beautiful swan, but—I just heard *ugly.*

So I thought I was. For years.

It wasn't until I was sixteen—fresh out of CYA—that I walked down the street looking for a job and multiple cars honked at me. I had never been honked at before.

Was I pretty?

As it turns out—*I was.*

Allie stared at my body, comparing it to hers.

"I would kill for your tits," she said, looking at me, then looking at herself in the mirror.

Fuck.

It seemed the green monster that lived in her was still alive and well. I brushed it off and slid the curtain open, stepping into the shower. Water fell over me in a cascade as I washed, conditioned and shaved. I expected her to join me, and when she didn't I peeked out of the curtain to find her sitting atop the sink, rolling the pipe once again. She was stuck.

"Allie ...," I called to her.

"Oh yeah! I'm almost done," she replied, blowing the smoke through her thin lips as she slid off of the counter. A knock came at the door.

"Yo! Whatcha'll even *doing* in there?! I need to piss!" It was Keith.

Allie's eyes opened wide. She snatched up her denim coat, shoved the pipe into the inside pocket and set it gently onto the floor before jumping into the shower with me at lightning speed. Once her feet hit the tub, she yelled toward the door.

"Sorry, Papa! We'll be out in a minute!"

"Ya'll been in there a fuckin' hour—Jeez! How long it take to wash your ass? Wrap—it—*up*!"

His voice held a hint of frustration. I would soon come to know that he was a fickle hand. He was frustrated often but it waned quickly.

Allie made hand movements, gesturing me to change places with her, so she could stand under the scalding water. I was done anyways. I shifted to the far side of the tub, opening the curtain slightly, to locate a towel. I stepped out, careful not to land on the denim jacket that was the holding place for our dope pipe.

Shutting the curtain behind me, I dried myself off enough to use the towel to wrap up my soaking wet locks and sit on the closed lid of the toilet. As quietly as possible, I felt around for the pipe. I could hear it *tink* against the floor before pulling it from the jacket and bringing it to my lips for one last hit.

Allie looked out of the curtain just as I lit it up.

"That's all I have so take it easy. We gotta make it last until I can sneak the car to hit up my dealer ..." I understood. I also didn't care.

I was an addict. I hit the pipe again. And, again. And, again.

Chapter Seven

Best Western, Redondo Beach, CA, May 8th 2008.

Keith sat at a computer, scrolling through a web page that I couldn't see. The light from the screen gleamed off his face, in an otherwise dark room. I was wrapped in a slightly too-small towel, scanning for my suitcase, the bathroom door cracked slightly, letting a waft of smoke slip through the thin open space.

I wondered if he could smell the dope seeping out from the other side. He must have heard me, as he looked up and gave me a slow once-over. I felt out of place and uncomfortable in an instant. I grabbed the edge of the towel wrapped around my narrow body and readjusted it, making sure all of my interesting parts were well shielded from his seemingly prying eyes.

"Hey," he said, low and calm, with an upward nod of his head.

"Umm—hey?" I replied.

I felt an unfamiliar tremor find its way through my voice. I was not a timid girl. I was direct and outspoken and I held my own—but in this instance—I was a child. I couldn't make out why my face flushed hot and red, and my eyes darted around the room, like a cornered wild animal, but they did.

Maybe it was because I was standing half naked in a room alone with Allie's boyfriend—something I was sure would set her off. I wasn't even remotely prepared to deal with that. Maybe it was the drugs, or my intuition. Or maybe—just maybe—I was a child somewhere down there beneath the layers of warrior shielding a hard life required I build around myself and in this moment—I lay bare.

Locating my suitcase by the door, I realized I would have to pass him to get to it.

"I just … I need …" I pointed to the suitcase.

His eyes undressed me again before nodding and refocusing his eyes on the screen. My feet found their way across the low, rough carpet and just as I was reaching for the handle, the bathroom door swung open and Allie emerged naked.

Naked and bald.

I adjusted my towel again before grabbing my suitcase and attempting to pull it back over to the safety of the far side of the hotel room. Her eyes followed me in suspicion as I made my way toward her. I brushed it off. Any reaction would imply guilt, so I had none. My nonchalance seemed to satisfy her twinge.

She trotted off toward her pile of clothes on the bed, without giving me another glance. I rifled through the suitcase quickly, searching for any two possible matching options of pants and shirt, then slipped into the bathroom to dress, reemerging just as quickly.

Allie was dressed and standing behind the computer chair when I reentered the room. She traced Keith's shoulders with her long acrylic nails, as she softened her voice into one I had never heard.

"Papa, let's go shopping …"

He spun the chair to face her and looked at her with a smile. He seemed to love her. I wasn't sure why. I thought he was much more attractive than she was and she was a raging meth addict but hey—who was I to judge.

"Ion know, man … it's getting late. Kinda wanna just chill." His quiet voice filled the silent room as I sat down on the edge of the bed.

"Papa, it's my friend's first night and I wanna show her a good time. We can get some champagne, I need some new shoes and Kay, well …" Allie gave me a look of pity out of the corner of her eye. "She needs some things."

I looked at my outfit. My baggy jeans and loose-fitting Norcal T-shirt were obviously not appropriate attire. There was nothing wrong with my clothes, other than that they were men's—a habit I had picked up while selling drugs. I'm not sure why. Maybe an attempt to look more intimidating. Keith gave me another once-over.

"Alright, babe," he replied with less of a fight than I had anticipated.

He stood up, grabbed his wallet and keys off of the desk and made his way out the door, without another word. Allie winked at me and pulled the pipe out of her pocket. At the sight of it, my eyes bolted toward the door with paranoia, expecting him to return at any moment.

"He's not coming back. He's warming up the car."

"It's eighty-five degrees outside," I laughed in reply.

"Men do dumb shit. I don't know, but he's definitely warming up the car." I laughed as she pulled the pipe to her lips. We each took a hit from the glass before stowing it away and heading out the door.

"Um, Allie?"

"Yeah."

"I don't have any money to go shopping."

"Don't worry, boo, I got it. You need something a little more—I don't know—*feminine*."

I looked down again briefly, feeling a twinge of shame and then headed for the car, missing Ericka in that moment more than I had allowed myself to in quite some time. Ericka would never have made me feel ashamed. If she was still here—I probably would've never met Allie at all. But she wasn't.

* * *

Skyway, Paradise, CA, May 2006.

Two months before meeting Allie.

You could hear the leaves fall through the deafening silence. The soft rustling of the branches waving in the rush of a crisp breeze. Chills found their way up my flesh, landing on the tip of my nose. I sniffled and swallowed, blinking slowly.

What just happened?

Shock froze the tears inside their ducts, not allowing them to fall.

I'm supposed to be crying, aren't I? Why am I not crying?

The weight of my body was suddenly too much for my knees to carry and beneath it, they buckled. I crashed into the gravel drive and found myself grasping at the earth, breaking it in my palms. So fickle. Mountains were nothing but tiny bits of dirt all smashed together. Separate the pieces from the whole and it would crumble in your hands. Each speck useless on its own. But together, they were what inspired awe.

She was a mountain. One he would die trying to conquer. Breaking her into little pieces until she was nothing but the dirt they would shovel on top of her casket.

Tell me it's not real. Tell me I'm dreaming.

I dialed my voicemail to hear her voice once more.

"Hey, Kay … um … I thought you were gonna go with me to Chico but I can't get a hold of you. I—I love you—are you mad at me? I—I hope you're not mad at me. Anyways, leaving now but call me when you get this. Love you!"

Click.

I wasn't mad at you, beautiful. I could *never* be mad at you. You were like the light that glimmered through the trees as the sunset. The human equivalent of dancing in the rain.

How could she think I was mad at her? That's the last thing she thought before she—

I couldn't say it. Still no tears.

Ericka's sister-in-law's voice bled through my eardrums just moments before.

"Kay—are you sitting down?"

"Why?"

"Sit down."

"You're scaring me! Just tell me what's going on!"

"Jeff killed Ericka in Chico last night—"

"What the fuck are you talk—"

"He followed her to Toys R Us, shot her five times in the parking lot and then turned the gun on himself—"

"This isn't fucking funny, Jennifer!"

"I would *never* joke about something like this." Her still, quiet voice came over the receiver again with a soft strength. Like the gust of wind that sent you over a cliff.

"I would *never joke*—about something like *this*."

"Where is Kelsey?" I asked, still not believing.

"She's safe. She was in her car seat when it happened. She's with us."

This precious, eighteen-month-old girl had watched both of her parents die in front of her. Ericka was four months pregnant with her second. Jeff was wanted for a conviction carrying a life sentence.

A memory resurfaced abruptly. A month prior we had gone to her old apartment where she lived with him to get the last of her things. He had left horrifying notes. Scribbled just so that you could almost hear the psychotic rage coming through the words written on the ripped brown paper of grocery bags, scattered around the disheveled apartment.

Chilling—like a scene straight out of a Quinten Tarantino film.

"I'm gonna kill you, you fucking cunt!"

"I'd rather die than go back to prison and if I can't have you, no one can."

When we went to leave, we were greeted by none other than, what looked like, the entire Chico police force, including their tactical team. The neighbors had heard movement in the apartment and thought it was him. We left after thorough questioning, without issue and Ericka went into hiding until the newness of the threat wore off. Or, so she thought.

I was supposed to be with her. I didn't answer because I was tubing down Honey Run—a well-known river in Paradise, California. I didn't have any phone service and didn't get the voicemail until the next day.

I hope you're not mad at me …

I looked up at the sky that I all but expected to crack into pieces and I grappled with my denial and grief. I didn't pray much but—it seemed like a good time.

I didn't pray to God. I prayed to her.

"Ericka, please—" The tears found their footing and began to roll. "If you can hear me—if—if you're still with me—please just—please give me a sign!"

A gush of wind thrust through the branches. Leaves fell in tens and twenties, being carried in twirls and swirls down the drive. The gust came again, this time stronger and I felt a warmth come over me and rush through my body like a burst of electricity. A peaceful and knowing calm entered my being like a warm hug. I vibrated as the wind continued to rage, scattering the fallen brown, orange and green. Swirling like my head. Falling like my tears. Cracking—like my heart.

Then—in a snap of a finger—it was done. The trees and time stood still, if only for a moment.

I looked up to the sky again to see a butterfly, floating and flitting in circles around me. I took a sharp breath and as I blinked the last of my tears onto my cheeks, it flew into the sun. I lost my best friend, but she was with me. She would always be with me. She just went—home.

* * *

South Bay Galleria, Redondo Beach, CA, May 8, 2008

The bright fluorescent lights at the South Bay Galleria beamed down on everything below as if a halo. The designer items sparkled with newness and I wanted to touch everything. Maybe it was the mind-altering substances coursing through my veins, but I felt like a balloon that had once been tied to a child's hand and now had been set free. Just a faraway dot of red being swallowed up by the blue. Drifting up and up through the vast open sky, only accompanied by the clouds.

Allie zoomed through the aisles, sifting through the items, before either leaving them lay or throwing them over her left arm with a swift toss. I scanned the racks for things that I might like. I wasn't sure what I liked anymore. My style was more or less of functionality at the present moment, but there was a time—during a two-year stint of freedom, before my inevitable violation—where I was actually quite the normal teenage girl.

My style didn't expand beyond Abercrombie tees and American Eagle skirts, but it was definitely a more girly vibe than I had going on at present.

"*THIS!*" Allie shrieked at me, "*THIS IS SO YOU!*"

She held up a pearl-colored, low-cut, baby-doll dress. I didn't know if it was me, but it was definitely more feminine. Allie grabbed me by the arm and dragged me quickly behind her toward the fitting rooms, stopping only to give the shoes on clearance a once-over, her bulging eyes falling on a pair of white, peep-toe, baby-doll pumps.

"What size are you?" she asked, rifling through the boxes.

"Umm … like a nine? I think."

"You think?"

"I don't know—is it different for heels? I'm five feet ten. Not really a big necessity for added height."

Allie tilted her head and gave a slight sneer.

"You don't wear heels for height; you wear them because they're fucking hot, OK?"

"Whatever you say, fairy godmother."

She cackled. Apparently she liked the term, and, of course, drugs made things more amusing than they actually were. She floated her finger down the row of boxes of her approved style and stopped two boxes before the floor.

"Nine!" she said before popping the box out from its place in the stack. "Come on."

We resumed the power-walk pace to the dressing rooms. As we reached the doors, she shoved the dress and shoes in my hands and pushed me forward expectantly.

"Go!"

"Jeez, crazy—calm down. I feel like I'm with my mother." I closed the dressing room door behind me with a quiet click.

"I'm a sucker for a makeover!" she called to me from the other side of the door.

Makeover. I scoffed to myself. *What makeover?*

I had already undressed and was slipping the dress over my head. Tiny beads of sweat formed at my collarbone in the heat of the fluorescent lighting. It fell perfectly into place. Next the shoes. I slipped my feet into the pumps and they slid on like a frame from Cinderella.

I stood. I turned to the mirror. I looked.

"*Wow*," I said out loud.

"Wow, *what*?! Let me see!"

I was looking at myself in the mirror but—I didn't look like myself. I didn't know who that girl was. She looked like she had never seen a sleepless night, out of fear that she may be raped or killed, as a runaway out on the streets. Like she had parents who raised her in a good home and said grace at the dinner table. Maybe she had a scholarship to some fancy college and she definitely had never been arrested, let alone done or sold illicit substances.

She looked like—*someone else.*

But she was me and had I seen her any place other than this mirror—I would not have recognized her.

"Let me *see!*" Allie demanded from the other side of the dressing room door.

I broke my stunned gaze from the looking glass, turned toward the shuttered door and emerged.

"Whoa!" Keith had probably located us by Allie's supersonic screeches. I didn't expect him to be there.

"Right?" was Allie's response.

"OK, I'm done here…," I said embarrassed and spun on my heels, retreating back into the dressing room. I liked my clothes better. They were unsuspecting. Nobody stared at me like I was an alien.

"No, no, no! You look beautiful! Sorry! Just a big reveal there, babe!" Allie said, laughing. "That's your look for sure."

"Yeah," Keith agreed.

I don't know why I didn't like that he agreed. I just didn't. Made me feel dirty. Like I did something wrong.

"Change back so we can get out of here. We're gonna go to Mik's."

"Mik the rapper?"

Allie laughed

"Yes … Mik the rapper."

* * *

SLAUSON AND LA BREA, INGLEWOOD, CA, MAY 8ᵀᴴ 2008.

The streetlights that lined Slauson Avenue flickered against the shadowy night, giving off a dim glow. It was late, but the City of Inglewood still hummed with most of its bustle. LA didn't sleep. In my hometown at this hour it would've been ghost, but it seemed to me that the energy of the city came in shifts. The early birds settled down as the sun set on the horizon and as they did, the night came alive with its other face. LA had an underworld, riddled with beasts dressed in the disguise of your wildest dreams, lying in wait to ravage the naive.

We stood on the stoop of the apartment complex, waiting for the buzzer. It rang. Keith held the door open as we slipped through and made our way to the back of the complex. Without a knock, Allie swung open the metal screen door into a run-down apartment.

There was a red "casting"-looking couch and a fake plant that was in heavy need of dusting. A small television sat on top of an ill-fitting stand, adjacent to the couch, but the living room was otherwise bare. The kitchen wielded off-white, peeling paint, stained from the tar of countless cigarettes and the table was surrounded by mismatched chairs and strangers, obviously a few drinks in.

Laughter filled the apartment and a plate of coke was making its way round.

"Hey!" Allie announced herself, strutting across the stained carpet, looking like a runway model for Kmart. There was a sure, crackhead confidence that brought it all together with a sort of sad charm. The darting eyes around the table made it quite obvious that she was the only one who didn't know she was three stories too high.

Not that I had taken the elevator down, I just had much more experience pretending to be sober.

"Hey, sis!" was Mik's reply. "I see you brought a guest with you. What's your name again, sweetheart?"

I went to answer, but before I could, Allie did for me.

"Her name is Keta!" The words flew out of her mouth like a tape in fast-forward. I had decided, a few hours into the bus ride, that the girl known as Katie no longer existed and officially switched identities the moment my feet hit the LA pavement. Growing up in foster homes, I had changed my name like men changed hats. Each new place, a new character. Hoping that I could outrun the shame that my real name carried in each of its letters.

Kay, Kate, Kat, Kaden, Keta. It was all the same.

I didn't care who I was, as long as I was someone else. Hearing the name Katie always felt like a punch to the gut. My hometown was the only place where people knew my real name and the only place I couldn't escape her.

The only place I couldn't escape—me.

It took Mik a second to fully register the sentence before he replied.

"OK! OK! Welcome to my humble abode, Miss Keta."

"Thanks," I said through a fake smile.

I didn't mean it. I wanted to leave, but it didn't seem viable. Instead I feigned interest in my cuticles to avoid conversation, which seemed like a good plan until it didn't work.

"Tell me something, Miss Kay." Mik had leaned closer.

"Yeah?"

"You ever sniffed coke straight off the corner of the brick?"

What an opening line. Nothing like it to make me feel right at home.

"Um … I don't think so."

"Here." He held a key holding a small amount of powder "Up, up and away!"

I bent over, plugged my left nostril with my index finger and sniffed with my right. It hit my brain and I was stuck standing in the middle of the kitchen like a character from an episode of *Looney Toons* with stars shooting out of my eyes and little birdies flying above my head.

"Hahaha!" Mik laughed loudly "That's good shit, huh? Betcha never had no dope like that before. Back in *Philly*, sis? *This was er'day.* Movin' birds in flocks!"

I didn't know what the fuck that meant, but I just nodded and smiled as he continued on about moving weight with some guy named Beanie Segal. Apparently, he was a rapper from Philly. Something about Jay-Z. I couldn't keep it all straight. My eyes were crossing from me being so high.

Allie had disappeared to the back room with a girl who didn't seem so happy that we were there and then emerged again before Mik had finished his long-winded war story.

"Kay!" Allie whispered from around the corner, waving her hand at me to come. I did.

"I'm gonna go with Ashlyn to go get some dope. Keep Keith distracted."

"What am I supposed to say? He doesn't talk much." I was annoyed. I wanted to leave and instead I was being pawned off on a group of strangers, while she went to get high.

"Just talk to Mik—he'll talk all night—just keep them busy long enough for me to go get some dope."

Allie whisked herself out the door before the word *whatever* could fall from my lips. I turned around. The kitchen table hadn't missed a beat. The plate continued to circulate. The air thick with smoke and stories all beginning with the phrase "back in the day." They were exciting enough to hold your attention—the first time you heard them. This was the first time for me, but definitely wouldn't be the last. The liquor kept pouring and before I knew it, I could have sworn I found myself having fun.

"Give the white girl a little white girl!" a gentleman at the end of the table announced.

The room roared with laughter. They must've been high as fuck, because it wasn't that funny, but I wasn't going to say no to another line.

"She's not white," said Mik with a wink. "She's just light-skinned. Ain't that right, baby?"

I smiled as I took the plate from his hand and inhaled the powder through my left nostril. I closed my eyes in reflex, as the coke hit the back of my throat. It *was* some good shit. As they opened, my vision aligned directly with Keith's.

He was staring at me.

"You thirsty?" he asked me.

"Um, no—I have some brandy."

I was confused.

"No, like—you want anything from the store?"

"I ... uh ..."

"Come on, we're going to 7-Eleven."

"Um ... OK."

His chair screeched across the linoleum as he stood up and I followed him out the door.

* * *

7-ELEVEN ON SLAUSON AVE, INGLEWOOD, CA, MAY 8TH 2008.

It was only a three-minute drive to the nearest 7-Eleven, but it felt like an eternity. I kept thinking about where Allie was and how she would react if we showed back up, together, with her waiting at Nik's apartment. I hoped she wouldn't care because she had re-upped, but I knew it was a fifty-fifty chance.

My anxiety came less from what she would do and more from what I would have to deal with. I hated when people made shit up in their heads and then I was the culprit. It had happened to me my whole life and I did everything to avoid it.

"We're here," Keith announced as he put the Impala in park.

"Yeah, I could tell because of the giant 7-Eleven sign," I replied, leaning forward to point at the beaming sign hanging brightly from the eaves.

"Oh, you a smart ass then, huh?"

"Better to be a smart ass than a dumb ass," I replied coyly, flashing a grin. I went to reach for the door, when something on the floorboard caught my eye.

It was the Koran.

"What's this doing on the floor? It's supposed to be on the highest shelf in the house," I said matter of factly, picking it up from the floor and holding it in his line of sight. The light, glowing red from the 7-Eleven sign, bounced off the green leather binding, making the gold Arabic lettering glimmer as it flopped over from its own weight. Keith stared at me for a moment, kind of dazed, before speaking.

"How you even know what that is?" he asked, not even attempting to disguise his shock.

"What's that supposed to mean? I know a lot of things, Keith," I said with a sarcastic sass, somewhat insulted.

"Nah—I ain't mean it like that, it's just—you know. Not a lot of white girls be practicing Islam, you know? Kinda caught me off guard."

The highest shelf in the car just so happened to be the dash of the backseat. I leaned through the small break between the front seats and tossed it gently to the opening between the windshield and backseat where it landed with a thud, inviting a smile of satisfaction onto my face.

"I don't practice Islam," I clarified.

"OK. Do you care to elaborate?" he said with a laugh. He was looking at me like I was an alien.

Why do people always look at me like that? I thought. It reminded me
of the way my mother looked at me and I hated it.

"Not really. It's not rocket science; it's public information. Read a
fucking book." He stared at me a moment longer, before breaking his
gaze and popping the driver's door open.

"OK, smarty pants. Let's go. Get what you want; it's on me."

The cool air of the 7-Eleven hit my face like a blast of arctic wind as I
walked through the double doors and the loud ding filled my ears with
sound, breaking up the Farsi chatter of the clerks. I wandered through
the aisles without a single want, but I knew I had to eat something
to keep from getting weird. It wasn't long before I loaded the counter
up with Sour Patch Kids, Cheddar & Sour Cream Ruffles and Diet
Coke and asked the clerk for a few crossword scratchers and a pack of
Marlboro Reds.

"You smoke them cowboy killers, huh?" Now it was my turn to give
him the alien stare.

"Cowboy what?"

Keith laughed and shook his head without explaining.

"Least I don't have to worry 'bout you smokin' mines. Pack of New-
ports too, man."

The clerk set the cigarettes on the counter and announced the total.
Keith paid in cash and we were on our way. I was halfway to the passenger
side door when I heard the word *fuck* fill the air.

I looked up to see Keith patting his pockets. He had locked the keys
in the car.

Great! I thought. *Allie's definitely gonna beat us back now.*

I searched my mind for a solution that didn't involve calling Allie but
came up short.

"Does Allie have another set of keys?" I asked.

"Nah, but my BM does."

"Your *what?*"

"Baby mom."

Weird acronym, I thought to myself, knowing that BM was the medical abbreviation for bowel movement, but whatever. Now didn't seem like the appropriate time for sharing more randomly accumulated knowledge. He anticipated my next question before I knew I was going to ask it.

"She lives around the corner."

"OK, cool."

Keith sent a text message then refocused his attention on me. I had made my way to the hood of the car and was leaning against it, staring up into the black of the city night. He followed in suit and sat just close enough to not touch me.

"How you like the city so far?" he inquired through a peculiar half-smile.

"I don't know—it's—*big*," I replied with a shrug.

"That's all you've gathered?" he taunted playfully.

"In my defense we're barely on hour ten and most of them were spent in traffic so—not a lot to go by."

"Ah, you do got jokes!" he replied with a cackle that bounded across the empty spaces of the parking lot.

"I do." I looked over at him as he chuckled. "How long have you and Allie been a thing?"

"Coupla months now it's been."

A couple of months? Allie made it seem like they were soon to be wed.

I tried to hide my shock and mustered my best nonchalance.

"Oh? She made it seem like longer," I replied, popping a blue Sour Patch Kid into my mouth to suck the sour off as I dug through the bag for another.

"Yeah, well—you know Allie. Everything is more to her than it is to everyone else."

I squinted.

What was that supposed to mean?

I had known a lot of men and had learned to read between their blurred lines. There was always a modicum of hesitation in believing that all of them were slimy, but the only thing I was ever wrong about was doubting my intuition. Just then a silver, '90s Mercedes SUV pulled into the lot.

"Ah!" Keith said hopping off the hood making a loud pop. "My baby moms."

Keith went and retrieved the key, hanging off the window of the Mercedes for a quick moment, before turning and heading back toward me in a light jog. The attractive Dominican woman in the driver's seat made sure to paint a heavy scowl on her face as she made eye contact with me before driving away.

"You ready?" he yelled from two parking spaces away.

I pulled my thin frame off the hood and made my way to the passenger door as I replied.

"If you stay ready, you don't have to get ready."

He chuckled, giving me a once-over before popping the locks.

"I like you," he said with a smile.

The sentence sounded innocent, but I knew what he meant and I had no intention of going there. I shook my head as I let a single word set a very necessary precedent.

"Don't."

Chapter Eight

Best Western Inn & Suites, Redondo Beach, CA, May 9TH 2008.

Water fell on my pale, trembling limbs as I stood in the shower with my forehead pressed against the cool tile. I was exhausted from a long night of pretending to sleep. The only thing almost as bad as not having drugs as an addict is being on copious amounts of them and having to feign sobriety.

Keith wasn't an idiot. I'm sure he had some idea we weren't fully straight, but I didn't want to rock the boat, me being a guest and all. Not to mention, I was pretty much fully financially dependent on Allie, so I was trying to keep it cool.

The water felt good on my skin. Lukewarm, on the cool side, to wash away the sweat of tossing and turning all night. I played with the stream falling from my nose with one of my hands. Catching it and releasing it again. Wasting time until Keith became a fully functioning part of the waking world.

I could hear them speaking through the door, so I figured it wouldn't be long until I could emerge my perky, energetic self and blame it on being the ever despised brand of *morning person.*

The talking took a dark turn into raised voices. My ears perked.

What were they arguing about?

I turned off the water and stood motionless, my fight or flight fully engaged. I couldn't make out the words. I slung open the shower curtain and ripped the white embroidered towel off the rack with excessive force.

The volume increased yet again, and I was almost sure I could make out the pronunciation of my name. I blotted my body with the towel as quietly as possible. Something crashed. I contemplated turning the water back on, but the thought was quickly thrust from my mind as an impossibility on account of suspicion.

I dried myself and threw an oversized T-shirt over my still sopping, wet mop of hair, letting the water bleed dark on the light blue fabric. I opened the door.

"WE JUST BLEEDING MONEY OUT OUR MAFUCKIN' EARS, YOU AIN'T WORKED IN *TWO* DAYS!"

Keith was screaming, in an obvious rage, as I emerged.

"ALL YOU CARE ABOUT IS *FUCKING MONEY!* I GIVE YOU EVERYTHING AND YOU CAN'T GIVE ME A FUCKING *DAY* TO FIGURE OUT HOW TO WORK THIS SHIT OUT? FUCK—YOU, KEITH!"

Allie's face was a deep shade of magenta and her eyes were twice as big as usual. She looked completely insane. Bald, wearing nothing but a pair of Keith's boxers and a somewhat see-through crop top, her wig in her hand, using it to gesture her outrage.

The door I had just walked through hit the inside wall of the bathroom and as it did, it clanged against the stopper on the other side. Two sets of infuriated eyes fell upon me and I froze. "THIS WHAT YOU WANT? FINE! FUCK IT. KETA—I'M A HO! THIS IS MY PIMP! YOU

EITHER GONNA WORK OR YOU CAN GET—*THE FUCK—OUT!* I'M NOT DOING THIS SHIT!"

What. The. Fuck.

I stood shocked for a moment before the words "*What the fuck did you just say to me?*" fell from my lips.

I felt far away. Far away from myself and the words I had just spoken. Like I was lucid in a dream, but it wasn't a dream; I didn't want to be lucid.

"You ain't have to say it like that, Allie. The fuck wrong with you?!"

I stared. Envisioning myself popping Allie's head off of her neck like a Barbie doll and tossing it over the balcony of our second-floor room.

"No, fuck *that* and fuck *you!* You wanted her to know. Now she knows. *Handle it!*"

The room fell quiet. The rage boiling within me wouldn't allow for words.

Well, when you fall flat on your face, you're not coming back here.

My sister's last words rang in my ears as if she were screaming them at me through a megaphone. I shook my head as if it were an Etch A Sketch in an attempt to make the cold hard truth erase itself from my mind but to no avail.

"*This* is why you brought me here, you fucking cunt?" I seethed, each of my words dripping with disdain.

"Yeah. I did. So either get on board or get the fuck on." So cold.

What had I ever done to her to deserve this? How could she? How?

It didn't matter.

"Alright! Alright! Let's take a step back—" Keith's words barely made it out of his mouth before I saw red. The room was a spinning blur as I lunged toward Allie, in an attempt to decapitate her completely, hate curdling my blood. Only one problem with my plan. Keith was in between us. I was strong but he was stronger. He used every bit of strength within him to hold me back, as Allie ran toward the door.

"SHE'S YOUR PROBLEM NOW, KEITH! FUCKING *DEAL* WITH IT!"

The room shook as the door slammed back into its rightful place, with Allie safe behind it. I melted into a puddle of sobs at Keith's feet, his arms guiding me down to the floor, as I collapsed in heaves. I bawled with my face pressed against the nylon floor. Shaking, sputtering and shuddering, realizing my worst nightmare.

Where would I go? What would I do?

I wanted to kill her. I wanted to kill him too, but mostly her. Keith backed away from me slowly and sat in the chair at the desk, waiting for me to regain my composure. I didn't.

"Hey—get up off the floor—get on the bed. You OK? It's gonna be alright."

He pulled me up by limp limbs and guided me the few steps to the unmade queen-size bed, where I collapsed again.

"I—It's—I—" I took a long ragged inhale and made an attempt to speak again. "What—*What the fuck*?! How *could* she?! I just—Ugh!"

I couldn't form a full sentence between the heaves.

"I'll buy you a ticket and send you back home." Keith's words were quiet.

"I don't—have a—home—anymore!" I managed to sputter between sobs. "I—have—nothing —now." Snot dripped from my nose, mixing with the endless flow of tears, making their way down my cheeks. I wiped my face with my palms before running my forearm across my nose until it reached the back of my palm. I tried to regain my composure. Took in a few shaky, deep breaths in a vain attempt to calm myself.

Get it together, Kate. Think. What am I gonna do? What the fuck am I gonna do?

I racked my brain for a number to call. Someone—*anyone*—who would care. That would rescue me. Anyone. There was no one.

With that realization, the dam broke loose again, and I was reduced to a pile of brokenness on a Best Western mattress. My stomach was tied in knots. If I'd had a genie in that moment, my first wish would've been that I could crawl into myself. The second, that one of those knots were a noose and the third wish would be—that I'd have no use for a third wish.

But there was no such thing as genies.

Keith sat quietly in the chair as my breath became less and less rapid. I searched my mind again for another way out. There wasn't one. There was a choice. One I had been faced with all too often in my brief life. It was one of shit or shittier. Bad or worse. A choice of life—or death. I knew I had found yet another rock and hard place and was being forced to reconcile with my fate. The only way to survive would be to make the rock or hard place my friend. See the bright side, however nonexistent. I would need to create a delusion of some sort, so that my fragile psyche didn't crack and crumble, at the foot of my newfound pimp.

Survival of the fittest.

I wasn't born the fittest. I was born soft and full of fluff. In need of love and security and reassurance, of which I was given none. Survival made me the fittest.

How did you survive? they would ask me. To which there was only one reply.

I didn't have a choice.

It's amazing what you are capable of when faced with no other option. Little girls don't go to bed at night dreaming of becoming dope-fiend hookers. When they ask you what you want to be when you grow up, the answer is always something completely out of touch. Astronauts, the first woman president, stupid shit like that. But life hands you cards and you either play them or they play you. Sometimes it's both but—better both, than having no wins to tally at all.

I processed the information the best I could in my chemically altered state, and as I sunk deeper and deeper into acceptance, my ragged inhalations became slower and slower. Soon, I wondered myself if I was breathing at all. Keith must've had the same thought.

"Hey."

I didn't respond.

"Hey, you good?"

I hated him. But I hated her more. I wanted to hurt her, but I knew he wouldn't let me and if I didn't play it smart, I wouldn't get the chance. I was playing chess now. Not that I hadn't been before. Life had always been a chess not checkers situation. I typically ran defense, as it was all I could manage. But, in this moment, I switched gears. I wanted to destroy her. Take everything she loved, like she just did to me. Keith had been eyeing me, so I knew that it wouldn't be too hard. But, I didn't just want to fuck him, stir up their emotions for a day or two, then end up on the street. That wouldn't do. No. I wanted to take him. Leave her with nothing but the wig on her head and a broken heart. Then, make him fall so deeply in love with me. So *fucking* deeply in love with me. Just so I could walk away and rip his fucking heart from his chest.

I wanted him to beg for me.

Until it killed him or he killed himself for not being able to live without me.

Maybe I had lost my mind. Good reason, I'm sure you'd agree, no?

His voice echoed again, breaking my sinister hatching.

"Hey."

I sniffled

"I—I have nowhere to go—"

"You can stay here, baby."

Fucking chump. I didn't respond.

"Hey … Hey—*it's OK!*" I felt a hand on my foot. At that moment I realized all I was wearing was a T-shirt. Face planted on the bed, my legs just uncrossed enough that you could almost see in between them. At that thought, I strategically pulled my right leg up just slightly higher, to show a little more flesh.

He noticed.

The hand on my foot became fingertips that traced their way up my leg, stopping just below the crease of my left cheek. Easy target. But hey, who was I to talk? He began massaging my hamstring, asking if it felt good. It didn't. I nodded.

The next moment he was on the bed with me. Exploring my body with the utmost curiosity. I arched and gasped, making him breathe heavier as he pressed himself into my hip.

"I *want* you," he whispered in my ear.

"*Then take it*," I replied cold.

He groaned under his breath.

"Oh yeah?"

Hot breath on my neck. I was wet. Not from attraction. From revenge.

Hell hath no fury—you know?

"Yeah."

The words were barely out of my mouth before I was ripped up off the bed into a standing position, his body pressed hard into my curves. He tore my shirt over my head in one swift motion and our bodies melded together, as if night and day had just been reunited after an eternity of being apart. Always just a sunrise or sunset out of reach, but never to meet. He ripped the magnum foil open with his teeth and grabbed me by the neck, tossing my upper body forward like a rag doll, leaving me standing, with my face pressed against the rumpled sheets.

He entered me. Hard. I gasped.

He slammed himself into me again. And again. I buried my face into the mattress to quiet my cries and he buried himself into me like a battering ram. He was hungry. Selfish. An addict. Just like me. But my addiction was to escaping reality and his was of flesh.

My flesh.

And, an addict always comes back.

I knew I had him before I did. He had no idea what he was in for.

He fucked me until he came and then collapsed on the bed beside me. A single tear found its way down the bridge of my nose before making its salty-sweet way into my open mouth.

I swallowed twice—and smiled.

* * *

VENICE, CA, MAY 2008.

The days folded into one another without leaving so much as a crease on my memory. My recollection of the weeks to come was more of a collection of fragments, blurred and glued together by substances, but there was one frame I'd never forget. This day—was forever etched into the wall of my mind.

The day I sold my body for the first time.

"You ready?" Allie asked me.

I had shoved all of my bitter hate down into the core of my blackened soul for the time being. I had to be cool. Play nice. It would all unfold perfectly and I would destroy her, but for now it was keep your friends close and your enemies closer.

Patience is an undeniably useful skill. One that I had learned plenty well, for obvious reason. It was Allie's arrogance that saw her to her end. I'm not quite sure how she believed that I was down with the whole fucking me over and stealing my self-worth by putting a price tag on my vagina thing, but maybe she had to believe it so she could live with herself.

Either way, she underestimated me and I was happy to let her.

I never meant for things to happen this way; you're my friend first.

The words went in one ear and out the other. Friend. She wasn't my friend. Friends don't traffic their friends. Pieces of human shit do.

She was vehement about the fact that this wasn't the typical pimp and ho structure. I was not under any circumstances to sleep with *her man*. But, all that did was confirm that my initial plan was an appropriate vengeance.

Silly girl. All is fair in love and war.

"As ready as I'll ever be."

Keith pulled onto the street and parked a block and a half up from the address, as not to be seen by the clients. I grabbed my small purse and my chirp and exited the vehicle. Allie stumbled her chubby, pale cankles up the cobblestone drive leading to the house, where a tall Mediterranean man answered the door.

"Hey, babe!" Allie greeted him in a disgustingly sweet tone.

"Hey, doll."

He gave her a kiss on the cheek, then looked at me. I must've been standing there doe-eyed because he opened the door a little wider and said, "I don't bite," with a flash of his perfect pearly whites.

He was attractive. Very attractive. What in the world was he doing hiring us? Surely he could get laid without compensation. All of my preconceived notions were smashed in an instant as I nervously entered the room.

"Hey!" A second man entered the room. "Welcome to Sebastian's bachelor party!"

The handsome man was obviously Sebastian. Not Sebastian was shorter, out of shape and slightly balding. Not ugly—just—not Sebastian. I suddenly wondered how we would decide who would sleep with who.

"Alright, bachelor boy, which one do you want?" chirped not Sebastian.

Ah … so they pick. I guess that makes sense, seeing as they are paying customers.

"Her," Sebastian said, staring at me.

A wave of relief fell over me. Not that the anxiety wasn't beating a hole through my chest, but it was just that, well—I would've slept with Sebastian. For free. Had it been the right situation of course. Spending most of my juvenile life incarcerated kept me pretty chaste. I lost my virginity only a year and a half before to my first love, then quickly violated parole and was locked up for the better part of the next year. I could count my sexual partners on one hand, not using all of the fingers.

I had been somewhat proud of that, for some patriarchally, brainwashed reason, I'm sure. But now … I didn't want to think about that. *Think about anything but that.* Sebastian grabbed me by the waist.

"What's your name, sweetheart?"

And another name to add to the pile.

"Ryen … with an E." I tried to smile as I spoke but am not entirely sure I was able to manage.

"You're gorgeous, Ryen with an E."

I smiled for real.

"Thanks, Sebastian with a—"

"Sebastian with a nice hard cock ready for you."

Gross. I'm sure if he knew it was my first time, he would've been softer. Not so vulgar. But maybe not. What good would telling him do? He grabbed my ass and pulled me closer to him. Just then Allie interrupted.

"OK! Let's get the donation settled before we get all crazy, boys."

"Ah, yeah … what is it? Five hundred?" said not Sebastian.

"Each," Allie replied with her palm out.

"I'll just put this here."

Not Sebastian counted out ten crisp hundred dollar bills and set them on the TV stand, half a foot away from Allie. I was picking up that there was some code to the whole thing, as Allie took the slight step toward the cash, grabbed it and shoved it in her clutch.

"Where were we?" Sebastian said, staring into the cornflower of my irises.

"We were …" The end of my sentence was swallowed up by his mouth as he shoved his tongue down my throat. I kissed him back.

"HEY!" Allie yelled our direction, interrupting the union. "*No kissing!*"

No kissing. OK, bitch, the rules would've been more useful beforehand but, whatever.

It's not like I cared about the mood. I had seen *Pretty Woman* a hundred times but didn't know the no kissing on the mouth thing was an actual thing. Apparently it was. Without warning, a knock came at the door and everyone froze.

Suddenly, I was free. Sebastian held his finger to his lips, indicating silence, and pointed to the hallway with his other hand.

I was about to have a panic attack. We crept into the hall.

"Shit! It's my fucking fiancé!"

Women's intuition never failed to amaze me. I was sure she would've been able to hear my heart thumping in my chest, had it not been for her incessant banging, drowning out the sound. The knocking stopped. A shadow cast onto the window and then made its way around the house, stopping periodically to bang on each separate glass surface, before reaching the back door. She knew we were in here and wasn't giving up.

"Maybe we should sneak out the back …," I whispered.

"Fuck, No!" was his under-breath growl of a reply. "She'll go—just stay quiet."

It seemed like an eternity standing in that hallway, not sure whether or not I was breathing too loudly or if at all. Then silence, followed by the click of heels down the walkway and the opening and slamming of a car door, before it revved and skirted out of the driveway.

"We're good," Sebastian assured us, not so convincingly.

"I don't know—what if she comes back, dude? I'm not down to get into a knock-down-drag-out with your fiancé today."

"No, it's cool, she's gone, she won't be back."

"I … I don't know …"

I was itching to find a way out of there without having gone through with the single most degrading act of my life, but I was grasping at straws.

"Shhhh—shhhh, babe. It's good, don't worry, she's gone. It's fine, see."

He pulled the blinds down and peeked out, pointing toward the driveway where her car had pulled up moments before, without any of us noticing. I began to refute, but Allie was already making her way down the hall, not Sebastian close in tail.

"Come on, babe," he beckoned, wrapping his arms around me to guide me toward his bedroom. He slid the thin strap of my dress off my shoulder and kissed it. Suddenly my vision went black. The next thing I knew, I was sitting at the edge of the bed, fastening my shoe. I didn't know what happened or how long I had been there, and I was grateful for that. I took a deep breath in and a knock came at the door.

"Ryen! You done?"

"Yeah, she's done, just a sec …" Sebastian answered for me. He was still naked as he swung open the door to face Allie.

"Nice cock," Allie joked as I stood up from the mattress, wobbling in my heels, my hair a disaster.

"We're gonna freshen up real quick; then we'll be out of your hair."

I said nothing as I made my way to the door.

Allie reached out, took my hand into hers, and gently pulled me behind her into the powder room. I sat down on the toilet in a silent daze as she popped the lock in place, before reaching into her clutch for the dope pipe. She went to lift it to her lips but stopped. She gave me a solemn once-over, then placed it and a pocket torch in my shaky, damp palm.

She must have known the feeling. Maybe she had a bit of remorse. She couldn't take it back now, but she could help numb the feeling a bit. In that moment, she showed a twinge of humanity. I mean, as much as you can show to the friend you just sold to the highest bidder, but hey. Beggars can't be choosers, right?

"Thanks, Al …"

I hit the pipe as hard as humanly possible and sighed a cloud of relief as she replied.

"Anytime, Kay."

Chapter Nine

QUALITY INN & SUITES, TORRANCE, CA, JULY 2008.

That first time was the one time I held emotion within me about sex work. It was as if in selling my body, I sold my soul. Once you've done something once, it was within the realm of possibility for you. Things that had once never been a second thought were now your daily routine.

Maybe I disassociated.

Drugs definitely helped with that. Symptoms of PTSD aided as well, I'm sure. It became a game.

It was the only way I could wrap my mind around the hell that my reality had become. I had thought I had been to hell and back before. I had mapped out the blueprint and knew it like the back of my hand. I could tell you just where to turn to get to pain of unknowable proportions. Just take a quick left after abandonment, straight past tragedy and if you hit addiction—you went too far.

I had seen hell, but there were levels to this shit.

I had only seen the first two floors, then got stuck on the elevator and there are no buttons to press, no escape route. You're just stuck, until it decides to take you back up, and pray you don't miss it. It doesn't return to the ground floor often. I must've miscalculated a basement run for a ground lift, because I was in the realms the demons lurk and it was dark here.

My joy came from three sources: drugs, fucking with Allie's head and making her look like a complete psychopath, and writing songs. I had a lot of time locked away in hotel rooms on my own and when I'm alone—I write. It had been my coping mechanism my whole life.

Locked away in my room, for months on end, ostracized from whatever family I was currently burdening? Write. Locked in a cage at a juvenile detention center? Write. Locked away in a hotel room, waiting for the next trick to come take another piece of my sanity. Write. Writing music silver lined my shit life, all of my shit life. I held on to it and it held on to me.

I didn't keep track of the days anymore. What was the point. Every day was the same. Drugs. Craigslist ads. Countless, faceless faces and roses on a nightstand. More drugs. More drugs. Repeat. Sometimes the rooms would get "burnt" and cops would show up, but I would just lock the door and be quiet until they left then make a break for.

I knew a thing or two about my rights, growing up in the system and, luckily, never was arrested for solicitation.

Allie *wasn't* so lucky.

We weren't sharing rooms any more. Keith tried to do the whole coexistence thing, being it was less overhead, but after I almost murdered Allie for the third time, he realized it best to separate us. The first two times she tried her luck, he intervened. I tried to keep my finger off of the trigger as best as humanly possible, but after I realized I made twice the money Allie did, I stopped giving a fuck about keeping the peace. Keith wasn't going to let me go. The third time she pulled some shit thinking

Keith would run interference for her again a twist of fate left her with a deep sense of regret.

I had thickened the plot in my little ruse to destroy her. I posted ads for her for in-calls and posted mine—only for out. Meaning, she got calls to meet tricks at the hotel and I got calls for tricks at their high-rises in Santa Monica and mansions in Laurel Canyon.

Keith was our driver.

They barely saw each other. All the while, I was generally unproblematic. Allie, on the other hand, had started shooting dope as opposed to smoking it, in all her free time and was losing her fucking mind. Every time we returned, from a sometimes eighteen-hour outcall shift, she would throw a tantrum.

Enough to make a man go mad. I was delighted.

But, upon this specific return she had lost her shit completely and chucked my MacBook at a wall. I came back to its shattered screen and a note.

"Don't touch my shit. Or my man, you fucking cunt."

I was done.

"Keith, I'm gonna kill this bitch when she gets back and if you get in my way—*I swear to God*."

"No, you're not! Just chill the *fuck* out!"

"No, *you* chill the fuck out! I'm—Fucking—Done! Do you hear me? This shit wouldn't have happened if you let me beat her ass the first time. Bitch would've got *checked* and not have all this false security because she knows you're gonna stand in the way. This ends—or I'm out!"

"I say what happens here. You hear me? *Me.* So you chill the fuck out and *I'll* deal with it!"

"No, the fuck you won't! You say that and ain't shit changed, or this wouldn't have fucking happened, Keith! Stand in the way or don't. Fist are flying the moment that bitch walks through the door, so you can catch 'em if you want or you can let me handle my business. *Point. Blank. Period.*"

"You talking about me ho!" Allie's voice came through clear as the door ricochet off of the baseboard.

"Yeah, bitch! You better pray to whatever god cursed this earth with your pointless existence, because you are fucking *dead!*" I snarled in disgust.

I closed in on her Keith still between.

"Whoa! Whoa!—" Keith's words didn't make it through my ears and into my brain. I had murder on my mind and it was a full block. I pressed my chest against Keith's, as Allie spouted off some oh-so-brave remarks, from behind him. "*Keith!*" I growled. "*Fucking—move!*"

I had never spoken to Keith like this. Maybe he didn't want to test the limits of my insanity. Maybe he was just sick of her shit too. But, with that, he left his captain-save-a-hoe post and made his way to the door.

"Fuck this, I'm out—Ya'll figure your shit out—*I'm done!*"

Oh, the fear that cloaked her face was a sight to marvel at. Her large blue eyes widened, until her lids disappeared beneath them, as she realized she was fully at my mercy.

"KEITH! SHE'S SO MUCH BIGGER THEN ME!" she screamed after him, with a thimbleful of hope that he would turn around and save her. I'll never forget the smile that crawled onto my face to live, as she realized the only thing between us now was eighteen inches of hate-filled air and the cruel sentence that escaped my lips next.

"Yeah, bitch—*I am!*"

I snatched her up by her hair so quickly she didn't have time to react and my fists started to fly. Every ounce of pain I had buried beneath the grave of my soul was taken out on her face. Even I was caught in the whirlwind of my fury. Spinning around the room, like a violent Tasmanian devil, leaving a trail of devastation in my wake. The microwave and mini fridge were displaced feet away from where they sat moments before. Lamps crashed into her head and then on the floor. It was only moments, before the coward curled herself up into a pitiful ball on the floor, begging for mercy and my character wouldn't allow me to continue.

Why?

Because I saw it as weak. Something she would do. If it had been any other circumstance, I would have never even thought of fighting her again, knowing I would win. But, this punishment was well deserved.

Be careful who you fuck over, they just might fuck you up.

I stood up from the shaking mess that was huddled in a corner, covering her head with both of her arms. She lowered them just as I spit in her face, saying words so cruel, I hardly realized it was my lips that had spoken them. *"You—are fucking—disgusting! Kill yourself bitch!"*

Just then Keith ran through the door.

"Get your shit, they're calling the cops."

"Good, leave this bitch here to rot—stank ass ho."

"Cool it. You got yours. Look at her. We're gonna get in the car and get her a room, then I'll take you to get yours. *Now!*"

Sounded like a good plan to me.

"This bitch is buying me a laptop."

"You can have hers—"

"*What?!*" Allie screamed from the corner.

"Shut up, *bitch!* Grown folks are talking," was Keith's quick reply.

I smiled.

I had been waiting for this moment for a long time. It felt better than I imagined. It wouldn't be long until she was gone for good and I could engage phase two of my plan. But for now—I was satisfied.

* * *

BEST WESTERN INN & SUITES, ONTARIO, CA, DECEMBER 2008

Allie was around a week more. Two max. She got arrested and I bailed her out, under the condition that she make herself scarce and never return. I thought it would be easy to close out on the original plot, but it thickened on its own, without any warning.

See the game is tricky. (No pun intended.) It's a living, breathing entity and it eats young souls for breakfast. Once it's got you in its grasp, it's hard to break free. The fast cash. Endless free drugs. (Which are the best kind of drugs.) My clients were millionaire crack heads and they paid well and came back often. There wasn't a drug I wouldn't do. I was slipping, slipping slowly. Losing touch with reality or any thought of escape.

I had formed some sort of weird bond with Keith. He was utterly in love with me and I—well—I had Stockholm's, apparently. It became easier to manipulate him, which gave me a false sense of power. We fought but not often. There were other hos, who came and went with a quickness, once they realized they couldn't compete, which only led to the ego trap of being the "Bottom Bitch."

I was lost in it all.

I called my biological family every once in a blue moon, and sent money home for my nieces' and nephews' school clothes and birthday gifts. I had repaired my relationships with my sisters as much as you can from a few phone calls a month.

They had no idea.

I could have left at that point. I'm almost sure of it. But, I couldn't. I was stuck in a time loop. It was physics, or psychology, or both and I couldn't escape it. I'm still not sure how I didn't die. No human body should be capable of withstanding that kind of chemical abuse. My dad was a seasoned junkie who still stumbled around the living plane, so maybe I had a genetic predisposition to be able to consume cocktails of illegal chemicals and live to tell the tale. Or maybe I did die. Maybe I died many times and my death was just a wormhole to another dimension where I would continue out my days. Either way, I was still breathing. I probably wouldn't be for long if I didn't quit soon, but I had no plans to do so. Keith tried to get in the way of me and drugs a few times, but I would just refuse to work and he would give in easy.

Until he didn't.

* * *

I was itching for a fix. I never fiend anymore. I had gotten used to the frequent influx of party favors that padded my will to live, but it had been a slow week. Holidays tended to bring business to an almost screeching halt and had I anticipated the drop in 3 a.m. calls to crack mansions—I would've stocked up, but being I was as high as a giraffe's ass, I hadn't given it a single thought.

"I'm sick of this shit, Kay … this dope shit is fucking with your head. It stops now."

"If I'm not high, I can't work," my flawless rebuttal came without missing a beat. "It's the yin to the yang."

"I'm not taking you to get dope."

"Then I'm not working—"

Everything was going in typical order. We had this fight every week. Keith's greed superseded him and he gave up the first time I didn't answer the trick burner. But not this time.

"I don't fucking care. I'm *done*. We only fight about *this*! It's—done! I can't watch you do this to yourself anymore!"

"Don't act like you fucking care about me! You pimp me out, take my money, stick your dick God only knows where behind the facade of '*knocking a new bitch*'—You couldn't give a single fuck about me! You want the gravy train to ride—*it needs gas*."

"I don't care about the money! *I love you, Kay!*"

I shuddered. Love me. He didn't love me and I definitely wasn't going to say I loved him. For me, saying those words was comparable to licking a razor.

The air chilled at the breath of my response.

"Don't fucking say that to me!"

Why did it matter? Wasn't this what I wanted? To make him fall madly in love with me so I could make him feel what I had felt? Used? Betrayed? Manipulated and devastated?

My act of rage didn't hold the foresight to cross the finish line, as I had once hoped. It felt wrong, dirty, degrading. I felt—ashamed.

It wasn't supposed to happen like this. Not like this. I wasn't supposed to care.

"I FUCKING LOVE YOU, KAY! THIS AIN'T NO PIMP AND HO SHIT NO MORE! I LOVE THE FUCK OUT OF YOU AND I'M JUST SUPPOSED TO ACT LIKE THIS IS OK, UNTIL I WAKE UP NEXT TO A DEAD GIRL?! NAH, MAN, NAH! I CAN'T WATCH YOU DO THIS TO YOURSELF ANYMORE!"

"THEN LOOK—AWAY!"

"I CAN'T!"

Keith threw his phone at the wall in response to his feelings of powerlessness. I froze, stunned. I'd never seen him act this way. He was quiet. Rarely yelled. Handled disagreements in a very matter-of-fact, strong-handed way. I had broken him down, little by little, until he was this shell of himself that stood before me, pleading with tears in his eyes.

"You're gonna fucking die, Kay ..." he said quietly, trying to mask the quiver in his voice. Those words hit my soul like a ton of bricks and lifted the weight of the world off of me in the same motion. Nothing penetrated my walls before—but this. This—I broke.

Into a million pieces. In a million worlds. I broke.

I was reduced to a crumpled pile of girl on the hotel bathroom floor, a strong sense of déjà vu, floating through the air. I sobbed and sobbed. Keith got on the floor with me and held me as I came to. The demons let go for a moment and I was human again. Coursing through my veins were the decades of pain and trauma I had been masking. It was a torturous and agonizing defeat. My gut churned and I convulsed in full breakdown and he held on to me.

Tight.

"We're gonna get through this. We gotta get through this."

"What if I can't do it?!"

"You can. You have to believe you can."

"I've tried before, Keith!" I cried between gasps. "I *fail!* Every. Fucking. Time." I collapsed in sobs again.

"You can do it this time—I'm here!"

Sudden rage filled me to the brim.

"I CAN'TTT—I FUCKING CAN'T! JUST LET ME DIE—I WANT TO FUCKING DIE. THEN THE PAIN WILL STOP! WHY WON'T YOU JUST LET ME DIE?!"

Keith's face was streaked with tears, holding on to me tighter and tighter as I tried in vain to escape his grasp as my demons took hold again.

"NO! DON'T FUCKING SAY THAT. YOU'RE NOT GONNA FUCKING DIE ON ME. DO YOU HEAR ME? DO YOU FUCKING HEAR ME?!"

Keith took my face into his now tear-soaked hands and screamed directly in it.

"YOU'RE NOT GONNA FUCKING DIE! SAY YOU'RE GONNA BEAT THIS—SAY IT!"

I slumped in his grasp, my pieces breaking into fragments of themselves. A newer low, every moment that passed. I sobbed.

"Say it!"

"I'm gonna beat this."

"Say it again!"

"I'm—I'm gonna beat this."

He kissed me and I felt something stitch together within my heart. This was not a part of the plan. I felt emotions for the first time in months, although one I had never felt before.

Was it love? Was it relief? What was it?

Oh … that's what it felt like for someone to fight for you. That's what it felt like to not be thrown away at the first sign of trouble. To not be abandoned. Discarded. That's what it felt like for someone to see through all of your problems, to the good of you, and think you may just be worth the fight—

I had never felt that before from anyone other than my sisters. It felt good. It felt like what I had been missing. Maybe I did love him, but if I did, why? Funny, that the most love I had ever been shown had come from this two-bit pimp.

It made me sad. Now I knew what it felt like, which meant I had something to lose. The way my life typically panned out if I had something to lose, I inevitably did.

What's that? Sleep? Sleep sounds good. I don't have to think when I'm sleeping.

I fell out on that bathroom floor and Keith gathered me up as if I were pieces and laid me in bed before he turned the lights out and breathed a sigh of relief.

* * *

HOLIDAY INN EXPRESS, ONTARIO, CA, JANUARY 2009

I walked among the living dead for the next few weeks. I slept for the first five days, in a lifeless coma, only waking when Keith would shake me out of my slumber for a meal. I would typically devour it in seconds with heavy lids, and then fall asleep among the fast-food wrappers.

I'd startle awake from time to time, in a sea of blankets and trash labeled *Jack in the Box,* thinking Keith had left. He didn't. He did take to the other queen-size bed to sleep for this period. But, he hung in there, waking me every once in a few days, trying to get me to rise from the dead.

At first he was gentle, but after a week and a half, he was losing his calm.

The thing about kicking stimulants is—if you don't want to wake up next to a dead girl, you're gonna have to live with the looks of one for a while. I felt like I had used the entire energy quotient for my ninety-year life span in the last seven months and there was nothing left to give. I tried to sit up and would slump over. My limbs were cinderblocks and my eyelids, stone. Sleep was my natural state.

This particular day Keith was done with the comedown and decided that I was too. Something hit me, waking me from my dream with a start. It was my phone.

"I posted an ad; you need to get up."

"I'm sleeping," I hissed in his direction.

"You've been sleeping for a week—*get up!*"

"How about—fuck you?" I snuggled deeper into my cocoon of blankets in defiance.

"No—*fuck you!* You said you were gonna try! This isn't trying—it's lying down!"

"Lying down *is* trying, you fucking dimwit!"

Keith shook his head.

"Don't call me out my name, Kay."

"I don't know what to tell you! I don't—*fucking*—feel good!"

"You gotta try—you can sleep until that phone ring but when it do—I'm waking your ass up. You gotta do something; you can't just stay in bed for a month. I'm not doing it."

"*Then leave!*" The words crawled out of my mouth like a demon from the underworld. Low and ominous. My gremlin was not happy and Keith was beyond pissing me off.

"Don't fucking talk to me like that, Kay."

I thought about getting up and throwing the phone in the toilet. That would solve my issue. But, that required an effort and will that didn't exist within me. I tried one last time to reason with him as I rolled over and pulled the blanket over my head.

"I'm not answering the phone; leave me the fuck alone."

"Yeah—we'll see," was his cocky response.

He thought he owned me. That he was my God.

"Sure the fuck will," I muttered under my breath as I fell back into the abyss.

It felt like only moments before I was shaken again and a Rick Ross ringtone filled the air. Keith was standing over me, holding the phone.

"Take the call, Kay."

"Fuck you—"

"NO, FUCK YOU! ANSWER THE FUCKING PHONE!"

The tone of his voice snapped me into consciousness. I focused on him with the glare I had inherited from my mother. I had always quivered when I saw this specific look. He didn't. I was out of cards to play. Maybe if I took the call, the guy wouldn't show, and Keith would shut the fuck up. Either way, I didn't have the energy to fight with him anymore. I snatched the cell phone out of his oversized palm.

"Hello—"

"Hey, is this Ryen?"

"Yes—"

"Are you available in thirty minutes?"

"Yes—"

"Where are you located?"

"Off the 10 and Archibald."

"Yeah, but where?"

"Call me when you get to the exit."

I snapped the phone shut and tossed it on the bed behind me.

"You sound mean as fuck!" He just didn't know when to stop and I could barely muster the strength to reply. It was like he was trying to exhaust me.

"Oh, I'm sorry, do you think I'm gonna hurt the trick's feelings? You sound dumb as fuck; now leave me alone."

Keith shook his head in frustration and before I could hear his further complaints, I was asleep again. Not for long. I was shaken awake in the

135

same annoying fashion, irritating my demons to the core. I'm almost positive, as my eyes cracked open, they glowered red. Keith. Again, with the ringing phone.

"Same number."

I snatched the phone from his hand, furious.

"Hello?"

"Hey, I'm at the exit. Where are you at?"

"The Holiday Inn Express."

"What room?"

"Call me when you're in the parking lot."

Click.

I needed to buy time. I hadn't moved from the bed or showered in a week. I needed to pull it together and fast.

"Get the fuck out."

"He's here?"

"No, I just don't like you anymore. Yes, he's fucking here."

"You gonna test my limits, Kay. I suggest you cool the fuck out with the attitude."

"You're getting what you want and it's not gonna be easy for me, so I'm not making it easy for you."

"You—"

I cut him off

"You want me to take the call or not, bro? He's at the exit. GET THE FUCK OUT!"

"I'M NOT YOUR FUCKING BRO. YOU LUCKY THIS CLIENT HERE!"

"Yeah, yeah, yeah."

I hated everyone—especially him. Keith looked at me with furrowed brows before exhaling deeply and walking out the door, slamming it so hard behind him the window panes all but rattled out of their grooves. I pulled myself up onto my feet and caught a glimpse of my reflection.

Fuck. I was a disaster. No. I was a train that wrecked into a disaster during a tsunami. How the fuck was I gonna pull this off? I ran to the sink and splashed water on my face before dousing a washcloth with hand soap and frantically wiped it over the most important places.

"A lick and a promise."

My foster-mother Argie's voice filled my head. She's the one who taught me the most about being a woman and was one of the few homes I actually fit in and felt love. We lived in a small house in Weed, California, where I was the only white girl. She had so much love in her heart. My foster-sister Tatiana ran away, back to her pimp, right before my county decided there weren't the appropriate "Mental Health Resources" I would need to live there. She was fourteen.

"A lick and a promise."

I called it a whore bath. Same thing. The phone rang.

Fuck!

I rummaged around for a clean dress to slip over my head and snatched my hair up into a messy ponytail, combing my bangs to one side. They covered my left eye. I rushed to the bathroom counter and frantically applied eyeliner to one eye and a touch of mascara, hoping the bang would cover the undone eye. The phone rang again. I picked it up.

"Room 303."

"Got—"

Click.

I gave myself another once-over. I was still a train that wrecked into a disaster, but the tsunami was over and it would have to do. I ran around the room, straightening the disheveled bedspread and relocating trash to the bin, as a knock came at the door. I answered it. The young Asian gentleman who stood on the other side of the threshold looked frightened instantly, only uttering the words "Um—yeah, no," before spinning on his heels and retreating to from whence he came. I had never had a client walk out on me before. Not great for my ego, but I got it. I slammed the door behind him and dialed Keith's number.

"Yo."

"He left."

"What do you mean, he left?"

"What the fuck about *he left* isn't clear?"

"Fuck."

Click.

I hit the bed in a sigh of relief and was out before Keith returned.

Chapter Ten

It was another two weeks at least until I was back to a decent level of functionality. I still felt like death but each day, Keith pushed me a little more. We fought constantly the next few months, but if I'm being honest, if it weren't for him pushing me, I may have never gotten up again. I was that tired. And, not just from the comedown. From my life in its entirety. Why did everything have to be so hard? It seemed like every rock bottom had a trap door into quicksand. The harder I tried to escape, the deeper I sunk. Constantly caught in the throes of defeat, it wouldn't have been a difficult decision to just surrender and let it take me under.

I changed my hours from the night shift to daytime, as to avoid the tweaker scene as much as possible. I took in-calls instead of out. Mainly corporate commuters on their lunch and rush hour. Most of them wearing wedding bands that left a sick, sinking feeling in my stomach. It made me despise men as a species for the most part. Couldn't trust any of them. Not. One.

Night calls came too, but I'd turn off my ringer at about eleven o'clock. I was afraid. Afraid the wrong client would ring and the next thing I knew, I'd be sitting in a smoke-filled room with a dope fiend and all my hard work to get clean would be lost. Weirdly enough, during that six-month span, I didn't host a single junkie client. Party clients, yes. But not the crackhead millionaires I would encounter before. It's like there were none. I had put myself in a different auric field somehow and was being protected from the game's second layer of darkness that had almost stolen my life, not a full year prior.

The only catch was, it's hard to sell your body sober.

It ate at my core. Day in and day out. Each new client took a little piece of me and I feared that soon there would be nothing left. So I doubled down on my THC ingestion to take the edge off. It seemed to help but was a Band-Aid at best.

"Babe—"

The words broke through my daze and I was jolted back into reality. I looked toward the source of the voice. It was Keith. Of course it was. He did a good job of isolating his supply.

"Hey."

"Roll some."

"Yup—"

I reached for my oversized bag and pulled out a foil wrapper containing two blueberry swishers and a green pop-top bottle of the strongest indica strain the dispensary had to offer. I set the items on the crisp, white Hilton comforter and continued to rifle through my bag.

"What you need?"

"Something to break it up on?"

Keith reached across the desk he sat at and slid a losing scratch-off ticket across the table before tossing it in my direction like a frisbee. It spun as it landed on the bed, hitting my thigh.

"Nice throw."

"Kobe, man."

We laughed in sync as I proceeded to split the swisher with pristine care and broke down the weed into fine chunks. Rolling blunts was an art. Weed kept me sane, so I smoked a lot of it. I twisted and licked the blunt smooth, then ran a lighter over it from end to end, for good measure, before lighting it up. The smoke curled itself around my head like a halo and I basked in its wafting pungency.

"'Tis a fine flower," I said in an English accent, passing Keith the blunt as I coughed gently and then sunk into the bed.

"'Tis," he replied through his smoky exhalation.

Just then the phone rang.

"Hello?"

"Hey! I'm at the exit."

Fuck. I forgot I had someone coming. I motioned Keith toward the door.

"OK, I'm at the Hilton. Call me when you're in the parking lot."

Keith made his way silently to the exit.

"Will do!"

Click.

Keith took another hit of the blunt before knocking the cherry into a Coke can and heading out the door. I looked around at the room. It was in fair shape. *Mirror check. Not a hair out of place. Febreze. Perfume. Done.*

The phone rang.

"Room 217."

"Cool, see you in a sec—"

Moments passed and the expected knock came at the door. I swung it open with my smile painted on.

"Hey, stranger! I know you!"

It was one of my regulars, Michael. A tall, blond surfer lawyer. Great tipper. Typically, I'd go to his beachfront condo in Manhattan Beach, so seeing him at a hotel was a surprise.

"Hey, gorgeous!"

He embraced me in a sensual hug as I slung the door closed behind him.

"What was that number you called me from? I didn't see a contact pop up."

"Ah, yeah—that's my work cell."

"Little lunch break, stress relief for a change?" I said through a flirtatious laugh.

Michael and I typically spent our time with liquor flowing and lines a blowing. He'd keep me for hours, due to whisky dick, frequently racking up a bill of a few grand. Rarely did we actually fuck, because the blow and vodka mix wreaked havoc on his ability to get and stay hard, but when we did, I definitely didn't mind. A rare occasion with a john.

See I was sober, but not *sober* sober. My definition of sober was not doing meth. I'd still do any "socially acceptable substance" I could get my little sandwich grabbers on. Socially acceptable, meaning you could do it at a party without getting side-eye and whispers. Alcohol, weed, coke. The occasional pill. Ecstasy drained me of my serotonin and made me suicidally depressed for days after taking it, so I typically refrained. But, the other substances had minimal life-threatening side effects and therefore had been deemed acceptable by myself and Keith. In moderation of course.

Moderation meaning I was getting paid to do it.

"Nah ... I just got off and was perusing Backpage before I left the office and saw you were in the area. Best to go with tried and true," he replied with a wink throwing a stack of twenties on the nightstand.

"To start—"

"You're my favorite; you know that," I coyly replied, grabbing him by the tie and pulling him toward the bed. It wasn't three steps before I bumped up against the frame, halting my backward progress while his momentum continued, forcing his hard chest to crash into and wash over me like a wave. His large hand grabbed my throat and squeezed gently. I quivered. Michael was *hot*. With most clients I was robotic, just going through the motions as quickly as possible, half dissociated from reality. But not Michael. There was a chemistry that I quite enjoyed and Keith couldn't make me cum to save his life. Not that he wasn't capable. He was just—selfish.

But *Michael*. Michael's touch made me flutter and tingle in places that felt wrong. Forbidden. Which only made it feel better. I wasn't supposed to like his touch or get wet as his hand found its home around my throat and firmly persuaded my head to the side, his lips brushing against my neck. I exhaled and shuddered, my body going limp in his swollen arms. His beautiful mouth traced my collarbone, leaving a soft kiss every inch, as an ocean formed between my legs. He reached his hand up my dress and around my black lace thong with a gentle force. Not aggressive. Just commanding. Just enough.

It was hard to breathe. *So what. Breathing is overrated.* I didn't need to breathe; I needed to cum. His fingers found their way between my legs and a waterfall cascaded down my ivory thigh. Another heavy gasp escaped from my open mouth. I felt him instantly grow hard against my hip bone. He pressed himself into me with a groan before he tossed me back on the mattress, snatched me up by my ankles and swiftly dragged my body to the end of the bed. He smiled. I quickly pulled my dress up over my head, discarding it on the floor behind me with a flick of my wrist. Michael reached to my hips, taking the thin piece of lace separating him from heaven in the curls of his index fingers and slowly, very slowly, slid them down. His knuckles swept against my fair skin lower and lower before pulling them from around my feet, tossing them in the air to land on a nearby lamp and lowering himself to the floor.

"Mmm ... I love it when you get on your knees," I said with a deep draw of satisfaction.

"The only way to worship a queen," he said, eyes low, through a passion-drunk half-smile before taking me in his mouth. It was like he had a magic mouth. He didn't just eat pussy. He drank me. Fucking me with his thick tongue before sucking my soul through my clit and I shook as I came. Back arched, hands in my hair, gasping for air—came.

He kissed my inner thigh as I quivered, making my legs shake more. My breath slowed. Then slower. I went to inhale again but his strength stole the air from my lungs as he easily tossed me face down onto my stomach, still shaking from my orgasm.

I heard the crackle of the condom wrapper and seconds later, he plunged into me. My hands grasped at the comforter as my neck curled back in pleasure and I let out a long moan. Suddenly I was thrust backward in my mind, to a place I kept forgetting to remember to forget.

I was seven again. Standing eyes wide in a dirty living room, tears streaming down my face.

"*I SAID—DON'T—FUCKKKK WITHHHH MEEEE!*" The words came like a lion's roar and the fist flew into my stomach as it always did. Sometimes it came quick, but this time everything was in slow motion. The room spun as it connected with my gut, knocking me back a few feet, to land on the filthy carpet, gasping for air that wouldn't come. A large woman's frame towered over tiny me, in a drunken rage, as I stared up in terror, pleading with my lungs to inhale, to which they refused.

144

The woman was always faceless in my flashbacks, but I knew who she was. I'm sure she was seething, spewing vile, hateful words down at me with her thin pursed lips, but the sound had gone out on the frame. I could still feel the tears streaming down my cheeks.

No, wait. They're real. They're on my cheeks.

I snapped back into reality with Michael beside me, his hand caressing my face.

"Hey ... Hey—where did you go?"

I was horrified.

"Oh my God! I'm so sorry!"

"No, no ... it's OK—I'm sorry!"

"No, it's not you ... I don't know *what* it was but—it definitely isn't you."

"Looked like you went somewhere for a moment. A not so fun place. Does that happen often?"

Great. My trick is trying to shrink on me.

"Um, yeah ... sometimes. Typically not during sex, but—yeah ... sometimes."

"Do you ... Do you want to talk about it?"

"No ... no—I'm fine. Just ... embarrassed. This one's on me. Again, I'm—I'm so sorry."

I only offered because I knew he'd refuse.

"Forget about it, beautiful. Just ... know I'm here if you need to—"

"*Michael.*" I cut him off with a stern look. His eyes fell over me softly, bearing a mix of concern and adoration.

"OK ... well ... I better get going."

"OK ..."

He got dressed quickly as I wrapped myself in a towel, then walked him to the door, where he hugged me much longer than our usual farewell. Held me tight, then tighter, squeezing one last tear from my eye. It fell from my lash onto his shoulder before he released me, tossed me one last smile and let the door close quietly behind him.

* * *

Marriott Residence Inn, Temecula, CA, May 2009

My mental health was slowly declining. PTSD flashbacks and bipolar episodes not being uncommon. Growing up in the system, you tend to gather a myriad of acronyms associated with your name. PTSD, ADHD, BPD, BP1. The list goes on.

I hadn't been on medication since I was ejected from the state system, without so much as a "Good luck!" two years prior. I had been on and off meds since I was five years old, Cylert being the first. It was one of the first ADHD medications and it's now been banned in all countries. God only knows what it did to my toddler brain. I don't know what doctor looks at a five-year-old and thinks, "Oh yeah. Drugs for this one for sure," but here we are.

It was raining. It never rained in Southern California, but today was the exception. Keith and I were staying at a Marriott Residence Inn, near Temecula. We moved around a lot because it always paid to be the new girl in an area. This one turned out to be a gold mine, which meant I worked a lot and it wreaked havoc on my psyche.

"Ya phone ringing."

Keith's voice broke through the silence as I sat in my underwear, working on a new song, at the desk. I looked over at him unamused and switched off the ringer. I was in protest. One that I fully intended to be peaceful but knew wouldn't be. The plain words that left my mouth rang in his with a different tone.

I said, "I'm done today," and he—disagreed.

"We paying for this hotel room, so you ain't done until the phone don't ring."

"Correction—I'm paying for the hotel room. You don't pay for shit. I'm done when I say I'm done."

"You gonna piss me off, Kay."

"I don't give a flying fuck! Can't you see that I'm losing my fucking mind?! You can't tell?! It's not *blatantly* obvious to you?!"

"SHIT AIN'T PERFECT, BUT YOU CAN'T JUST QUIT!"

"THEN YOU POST AN AD AND SELL YOUR BODY, YOU FUCKING PIECE OF SHIT. I'M—DONE!"

My dog cowered, as I screamed. I had recently gotten a blue-nosed pit bull. Her name was Harlem. She stayed in the room with me when the clients came, for an added layer of protection, and was very well trained. Perks of the vocational dog grooming school I attended in CYA. She was pretty timid for a pit bull, but the clients didn't know that. All they knew was she jumped at my every command and obeyed. The fear alone tended to suffice.

"You know what?! If you're done—I'm done!"

Keith snatched the keys up from the nightstand.

We had taken my car. They were my keys. Mine.

Rage filled my every molecular cell as my face grew hot.

"FUCK YOU THINK YOU'RE DOING?"

"THE FUCK YOU THINK I'M DOING? I'M LEAVING YOUR ASS HERE!"

147

Keith closed in on the door, swung it open, and let it slam behind him as I struggled to guide my legs through pant holes, entering wrath of God mode. Keith had seen me in this place many times at this point, but only one other time was I physically violent.

About six months in, we had gotten into a screaming match in the car and he decided it would be a good idea to utter the words, "That's why your family don't fuck with you." The words barely left his mouth before my fist hit his face. Hard. I saw blood trickling down through the palms now covering his mouth and nose—and I ran.

I was sure he was going to chase me. He didn't.

I stood in the parking lot for five minutes, a hundred meters from the car, before approaching it again. Keith sat wiping blood from his nose onto his new white T-shirt, in the driver's seat of his Impala, breathing heavily.

I'm sorry ... I—I didn't mean to do that, but my family is off-limits ... I have a hair trigger."

You just punched me in the face, Kay." He was weirdly calm.

"Don't bring up my family. You don't know what the fuck you're talking about and if you do, I'm not responsible for what happens next. It's off-limits."

I was cold and matter of fact, but I felt horrible. It was warranted in hindsight, but I didn't like that there was a part of my psyche that acted on its own merit, without my consultation. It was like my hands were possessed. I didn't choose to punch him. It wasn't a conscious decision. It was a reflex. Not one thought ran through my mind between him popping off at the mouth and me popping him in the face. They were cause and effect. I promised him I'd never put my hands on him again if he promised to refrain from bringing up my family and Keith—well, he walked around with a black eye for two weeks.

Today was different though—I was raw and had been fighting with myself for the last few weeks. My mind was a dark alley no man would be safe to walk alone. Though I had learned to manage, it wore me down and eventually—if triggered—it would break me.

One of the things about borderline personality disorder is that its core trigger is abandonment. Although Keith was a pimp who used and psychologically abused me—him walking out that door with my keys in his hand—triggered that abandonment. I disassociated. I searched frantically for something to wield as a weapon. All I could find was a thick, chain dog leash. It would have to do.

I threw open the door and ran in a fury through the downpour to where my car was parked in the lot. Keith had just started the engine. My vision was blurry and my blood boiled. I couldn't stop the thunderous voice in my head that raged with vengeance.

He's going to leave me? He's going to leave me? In my fucking car? Fuck no! Thwap!

I threw the chain against the windshield, shattering spiderwebs into the glass. I could see Keith screaming something from inside, but I couldn't make out the words. He frantically attempted to lock the passenger side door, but he was too late. I flung the door open and was soon inside, tearing off anything that wasn't bolted down.

The top of the center console. The rearview mirror. The visor. All in pieces in the backseat while I screamed the exact words the voice in my head had been repeating.

"YOU WANT TO LEAVE ME IN MY CAR? THERE WON'T BE A CAR. I'LL BLOW THIS BITCH UP!"

Now—I've never seen myself in a psychotic rage, but—I've seen the faces of those to witness, so I imagine it's not the safest feeling scenario. Keith bolted, leaving the car running.

I should run him over—I thought, quickly followed by—*You'll go to jail.*

Jail was my safe word. I couldn't go back to jail.

Keith was screaming at me, his hands high in the air, gesturing through the sheets of rain.

"You're a fucking psycho!"

Click.

I was back in my body and I *was* a fucking psycho. I scared even myself. I walked around to the front of the car and collapsed, my back against the warm grill, as the torrents continued to fall on my face mixing with the tears that fell just as heavy. I sat there shaking, defeated. Keith must've seen the eye of the storm because he approached me now completely drenched. Slowly—but still. I sobbed. Soon he was crouched beside me.

"Hey ..." I didn't respond.

"Hey!"

I looked up.

"Come on. Let's get you inside."

I looked at him.

Why was he still here? Oh yeah ... I almost killed him for trying to leave.

Whatever. I was too tired to fight anymore. I let him take my hands and help me to my feet. We walked slowly back to the hotel room and shed our sopping wet clothes and dressed again in dry ones. I saw Harlem still shivering in the corner and went to the floor to sit with her as she mauled me with sloppy wet kisses, butting her head into my chest in an attempt to comfort me. I held her and cried, wondering who would be the first to speak.

Ten minutes passed in silence before Keith lifted his voice.

"This can't happen, Kay."

"Well it did."

"I know but this shit is crazy, man—I don't know, man—"

"You obviously don't understand the effect this occupation has on the psyche. You try it for a month. Come back and let me know how it goes."

"It's not just the ho shit though, Kay … this goes deeper than that."

I took a breath before speaking slowly, to ensure he could fully digest the words about to form from my lips.

"You have to have shit that goes deeper to even be in this ho shit. The ho shit is the product of the deeper shit—not the other way around. I been through shit, Keith. Shit you wouldn't have survived, I guarantee you. When you go through the type of shit I've been through. Survived the things I've survived, seen the things I've seen—it makes you sick. It rots your mind. Makes you crazy. Imagine not having control over what's gonna send you over the edge, because it triggered something you had repressed, and now you're left to pick up the pieces of the disaster *you* created out of sheer reaction. Like you shouldn't even try because you're just gonna build a castle on sand and every time you do, a wave just comes and washes it away, leaving you with rubble and no will to start again. Imagine how it feels to be me. The person who claims to love me forces me to sell my body over and over again. Imagine how that *feels,* Keith. You care more about the money than you do about my sanity and I'm sick of it. *Sick.* Some people get sick in their body. I got sick in my mind. And this"—I gestured around the room—"this is making me sicker."

"Well … people who get sick … they take medication … and they get better."

"I don't."

"How do you know when you haven't tried."

Heat welled up within me, but I was able to calm it by closing my eyes and taking in a deep breath. I exhaled, my eyes still closed. "Don't act like you know me, Keith—you know very little. *Very* little. You know what I've told you. You don't know what I've tried, so drop it."

He must've seen the rise and fall of my wrath and decided to quit while he was ahead. He wasn't ahead. But at least he wasn't being chased out of a car by a psycho brandishing a chain in the pouring rain. An improvement, to say the least. The room fell quiet. I leaned my head against the wall and sighed. Harlem was now lying in my lap; her legs draped over either side of my knees. I looked up at the ceiling and I was taken back, into another flashback.

* * *

RED BLUFF, CA, FEBRUARY 2002

I had recently been returned to the care of my biological mother and stepfather from foster care, against my best interest. My mom appeared to be doing well in life, but for me it was … well … just not the best place. I was eating dinner at the bar, as I most often did. I wasn't allowed to eat with the family because I was grounded. Again. I was always grounded. It didn't matter what I did—it was wrong—and I didn't know how to make it right. A few days earlier, I'd had my month-long banishment to my room extended for another week. What was my crime? Coming out of my room too much. I needed water and to use the bathroom. They said I was manipulating. In reality, I was on lithium. The most common side effects being increased thirst and frequent urination. Tell that to them though.

I was currently on a cocktail of four different psychotropic medications—Ritalin, Depakote, lithium and Prozac—and they made me sick, tired and foggy. I couldn't get through one day of school without having to go lie down in the nurse's office. Despite being on them, I was still always in trouble at home. Trouble in this house meant being ostracized completely.

I went to school. Went to my room. Came out for dinner—ate at the bar—then went back to my room for the rest of the night. For months on end.

Sure I was difficult. I had extensive trauma and the slew of medications that typically changed every two to three months made me extremely unstable. What could you expect by pumping an adolescent brain full of chemicals, never fully stabilizing, before rotating the prescriptions, yet again?

I had decided I was done taking them.

I had been hiding my pills for four days and refusing them at school during lunch. I thought my plan was going off without a hitch, until the phone rang. My mother answered. A brief conversation ensued before I heard footsteps head toward the kitchen where I sat dangling my feet from the barstool, playing with my food and stalling my inevitable return to my cage—I mean—bedroom.

"That was your school." She didn't look happy. She was scary when she wasn't happy. I froze.

"Ooh OK." I drew my words out, looking down at my plate, pushing my salad around with my fork.

"They said you're refusing your meds at lunch."

"I am," I replied matter of factly, trying not to let the emotion that was steadily creeping up boil over. My face flushed hot.

"Katie! How many times do we have to go over this! You need your meds!"

"HOW DO YOU KNOW THAT? THEY DON'T MAKE ME BET-TER; I'M ALWAYS IN TROUBLE! I'M ALWAYS GROUNDED! AL-WAYS! HOW DO THEY HELP ME?! HOW?!" I shouted in defiant rage.

"WE CAN GO BACK TO THE DOCTOR IF THESE ONES AR-EN'T WORKING BUT YOU CAN'T JUST STOP. YOU KNOW WHAT HAPPENED TO AUNT DOROTHY WHEN SHE STOPPED TAKING HER MEDS!"

I didn't remember Aunt Dorothy, but her tragic end haunted my family like a curse. Dorothy was my step-grandmother's daughter. She suffered with mental health issues, as did many of my family members. She decided to quit taking her Prozac and a short time later, she lost her mind. Gave her three young children sleeping pills, shot them all in the head and then killed herself. My grandfather found them.

"I'm not Dorothy, Mom! I'm not going to kill myself!"

"No, you're not—because you're taking your *fucking* meds!"

"Don't know why you care so much. I'm sure you'd be happier if I was gone," I tried to mutter under my breath but she heard me.

"THAT'S IT! YOU'RE DONE. ROOM. NOW!"

"I'M STILL EATING!"

She snatched up the paper plate in its blue plastic holder and tossed it onto the counter, on the other side of the bar.

"ROOM! NOW!"

I whispered the words *I hate you* quietly, as I retreated to my bedroom. I closed the door behind me and let the tears fall, as they often did, before burying my face in the pillow to quiet my sobs.

* * *

"Kay?"

The voice brought me back.

I was still sitting on the floor, Harlem dozed off in my lap. I looked toward the source of the sound. Keith was staring at me.

"You need to eat something. You haven't eaten all day and you barely ate anything yesterday."

That was the thing with mania though. You didn't eat. You didn't even think to. Sleep didn't come easy either. The not eating and sleeping made the mania worse, which made the not eating and sleeping worse, which could—and would—eventually lead to a mild psychosis. It was a sick cycle.

"I'm not hungry."

"You need to eat something; this always gets worse when you don't eat."

"No, Keith ... I don't need to eat." A sigh reflected my defeat. "I need a *home*. I need a place I can call home. I need more than this. I need you to be present. No more girls that just run through here, stir up our shit, then jump ship, leaving me to clean up the mess. I came out here to do music and I've done nothing. I need more or I can't do this anymore. *I give up ...*"

Keith took a moment before exhaling deeply, followed by a soft nod of his head.

"So we'll get a place ... and ... we'll get you in the studio ... we'll figure it out ... we'll ... ..." Keith trailed off, observing the obvious shock that graced my face. The puddles in my eyes had grown too heavy to hold any longer and shattered as they crashed to the floor as I replied.

"Don't say that if you don't mean it."

"I mean it. I'll call Coach tomorrow—he's got buildings in Hollywood and I'll get you some tracks to write to and—when you get a good one—we'll book you some studio time. But, studio time costs money, so we still gotta work."

I hated that he said "we" still gotta work, knowing damn well that meant "I" still had to work, but I was so stunned by his lack of rebuttal that I let it slide.

"No more other girls, Keith. You bring another girl home, I'm gone. I mean it. *Gone.*"

"OK."

I couldn't believe he agreed. Suspicion entered my mind but I knew only time would tell. I decided to let it breathe.

"OK."

With that I stood up, walked toward him and embraced him. He hugged me tight.

"Thank you ..." I whispered in a breath of relief. "*Thank you.*"

Chapter Twelve

INGLEWOOD, CA, AUGUST 26, 2009

Keith may have been a two-bit pimp, but he kept his word. It wasn't a week before we had a studio apartment in East Hollywood. It was expensive, being that it was smaller than most holding cells I had seen, but it was mine.

A large, wide IKEA dresser lined the back wall and a queen-size bed took to the back left corner of the front and that was all that fit inside of it. But it was *mine*. By the end of the month, I had a pack of tracks to write to as well. Keith use to work for Def Jam and had managed a few artists throughout his years, so he had some contacts. I felt hope enter my being for the first time in over a year. I clung to it like it was the side of the cliff I had fallen off. Scratching, clawing my way up from inevitable and certain death.

Tooth and nail, baby girl. Tooth—and nail.

It just so happened to be my birthday, so I had taken the day off to celebrate at Mik's. We parked the car in the first space available, which was at least a quarter of a mile down from the complex.

Street parking in LA was the bane of my existence. I was halfway through the long walk up Slauson Avenue, carrying two bottles of chilled Moët—one I intended to drink entirely myself from the bottle and the other for the house—when my phone rang. I stopped. Keith was a foot ahead of me but, noticing I was no longer walking behind, paused and looked over his shoulder. I quickly took the two steps forward to be at his side and pushed the bottles at him.

"Here."

I wasn't answering calls that day, but this particular call had a 530 area code. My hometown.

"Hello?"

"Katie!" a man's voice came over the line through a sob.

"Dad?!"

I thought for a sliver of a moment that he had remembered my birthday, which was entirely unlike him, but just as a smile began to make its way across my face, it fell slack with disappointment as he replied.

"Your sister!" Uncontrollable sobs came over the line. "Your sister kicked me out—I have nowhere to—go—"

It's my birthday. He didn't remember it was my birthday. He needed something. As always.

My dad was my child more than my parent. He struggled with addiction and extreme mental health issues, which were exacerbated by his constant chemical abuse. The giver of my dysfunctional genes. The gift that kept on giving.

Thanks, Pops.

"Wait a minute! *Slow down.* What the fuck happened?!"

The sister who had taken me in before my voyage to the big city had taken pity on my father and let him rent the couch under the condition that he stayed sober. He didn't. But, that's not why she kicked him out. She kicked him out because he stole money from her son's piggy bank. That wasn't the line he fed me though.

"She's just—hateful—I'm at a hotel—I just got my social security check. I can buy my bus ticket—can I stay with you?" Always the victim, that one. I sighed, frustrated.

"I live in a studio apartment, Dad—"

"I'll—I'll sleep on the floor—I promise you won't even know I'm there—just—I have nowhere to go, Katie—I have nowhere to go." Sobs filled my receiver and I fell silent.

"H-hello? Katie? Are you still there?"

"I don't have an answer for you right now, Dad; it's my fucking birthday and I'm not dealing with your drama today. Call me tomorrow."

"OK, I'll—I'll call you tomorrow."

I pressed end on my Palm Pilot, threw my head back and growled a loud sigh.

"You good, babe?" Keith said after giving me a once-over.

"My *fucking* dad, man. My sister kicked him out. Didn't even remember it was my birthday, just *'Help me, help me, I'm in trouble.'* I just … I don't know what to do with him."

"Well, what the fuck he expect you to do about it?"

"I don't know. I mean—I do know—he was asking if he could come stay with me."

"You told him no, right?" Keith said as more of a statement than a question.

"I told him it was my birthday and I wasn't dealing with it now and to call me tomorrow."

"Whoa, wh—" I cut him off.

"Keith! If I'm not dealing with it with him—then I'm not dealing with it with you. *It's my birthday.* Let it lie—*please*! I want to have a good night."

Keith sighed, knowing the discussion wasn't over but didn't press further.

"Alright ... if you say so."

We paused at the gate and I kissed him.

"Thank you," I said with a smile.

The buzz of the gate being popped filled the air, and we made our way to the apartment. Mik was the first to greet me.

"Well if it isn't the birthday girl! I got you a little gift. Not much, just a lil' some, you know, haha!" His cartoonish laugh cracked me up.

"You didn't have to get me anything, Mik—"

"Well, please do be aware, you will be sharing, cuz it may be August, but it's snowing in this bitch tonight!"

Coke. Of course.

I laughed. Mik was such a charmer. A born entertainer. He could tell stories for hours, especially if he had a little help from the blow fairy. Ashlyn—Mik's girlfriend—must've heard the commotion because she emerged from the dark hallway leading to the bedroom and joined us in the living room.

"Happy birthday, Keta Kay!"

"Awe thanks, boo!" I replied, embracing her in a hug.

Ashlyn and I didn't always get along. She was intimidated by all of the girls Keith brought in and out before me and was a friend of Allie's. One day after Allie had been arrested, Keith left me at their apartment, where

I passed out on the couch due to acute withdrawal. I woke up with her standing over me, punching me in the face. I was dead asleep when she attacked me. I came out of my slumber into a rage and put her through the front window.

It took a few months for the heat to simmer down between us, but we eventually made peace and a year later, she was one of my closest friends.

The bottles were popped and poured and the plate of white circulated as the tar of our cigarettes hung our laughter to the wall. Even the sky wasn't as high as I was. Not just on coke, but with joy.

Today was a good day.

We continued into the late hours. When the bottles were empty and the plate ran dry, Keith and I headed home.

Home. Such a funny little word. How could four small letters mean so much.

We went … home.

* * *

HELIOTROPE DR, HOLLYWOOD, CA, AUGUST 27, 2009

I awoke with a start at the ring of my phone, drool moistening the left side of my lip, leaving a small pool on the pillowcase my face had been firmly pressed into.

"Ugh," I moaned.

My head was pounding, a consequence of the birthday festivities. Keith stirred, a frown curled into his forehead.

"Who the fuck is that? What time is it?" he spouted with irritation.

I looked at the phone. It was my dad. I answered as quickly as possible, to make the God-awful ringing stop.

"Hello?"

"Hey, kiddo!" He was awfully chipper.

"Dad—it's seven in the fucking morning—I'm *sleeping*."

"Oh, I'm sorry … OK … call me back when you're up!"

"Goodbye," I said before hanging up the phone and burying my head back into the bright blue and green checkered IKEA duvet. My head was throbbing. I tried to fall back asleep, but the invisible marching band thumping their drumsticks into my temple wouldn't let it happen.

This motherfucker.

I tossed and turned for a bit before stumbling to the tiny bathroom to rummage through the medicine cabinet for some sort of pill form witchcraft to banish my headache to the depths of hell from whence it came.

"Babbbeeee," Keith yelled. "Fuck you doing, man?"

I sauntered out of the bathroom in my underwear and an oversized T-shirt, and swept up the water bottle from off the floor, next to the bed.

"Ty-ya-nal," I said, the pills still on my tongue. I threw the water in my mouth and tossed it back like a shot of whisky.

"Ah—want some?"

"Yeah," Keith replied, grimacing.

I took the single step back into the bathroom and grabbed the bottle, tossing it on the bed. I missed and hit him in the neck. I burst out in laughter, making my ears ring.

"Babe! Fuck."

"My bad."

"Well I guess we up now," Keith said before popping two Tylenol in his mouth and washing it down with a gulp of Arrowhead.

"Yup."

"That was your pops?"

"Yup."

"Whatchu gonna tell him?"

"I wanted to talk to you first."

"What's there to talk about? We live in a sardine can."

"Yeah, but—we're never here and—"

"Kay," he interrupted me, "I just don't think this is a good—"

"Just for a month … I'll tell him he's got thirty days to figure his shit out, but if not, he's gonna be out on the street, and I'll never forgive myself if something happens to him."

"There's no other option?" I could tell I was wearing him down.

"Not a free one. We could put him up in a hotel, but we're gonna be in hotels anyways, so I just figured … you know."

"I got a bad feeling about this."

"Thirty days. Then he's out."

"You promise?"

I kissed him.

"I promise."

* * *

SHERATON GASLAMP DISTRICT HOTEL, SAN DIEGO, CA, NOVEMBER 2009

My pops was on a bus that night, and the next day I would be picking him up from the same Greyhound station where my journey to Los Angeles began. He looked a wreck. I could tell he had been using, but it was too late to turn him away. Not that I would have. I knew the chances of him showing up in the shambles of full-blown addiction were high.

But, I had once been brought out of the depth of the same dark and held just the smallest sliver of hope in my heart that a little love could be the catalyst for his emergence.

On the long drive home, I laid out the rules for him. He had thirty days to figure out another plan. Keith and I were gone constantly, only coming back from time to time to get clothes or other necessities and check on the place.

Thirty days turned into ninety and though I could sense Keith was getting tired of the arrangement, he put up with it—until I didn't.

Currently we were in San Diego. The ceiling-to-floor windows of the Gaslamp District Sheraton gleamed as swells of sunlight flooded through them. I loved high-rises. Something about always having to look up to people, knowing they were better than me, my whole life. The simple act of looking down on the ant-like people in matchbox cars below made me smile so deeply that the upturn of my lips ran ear to ear and then down deep into my soul. I sipped an aromatic blend of organic light roast from what seemed to be a child's tea-party-sized china cup.

Who made these things? I would need at least four to even start to wake up.

I poured a second cup from the French press that sat on the white-linen-covered room-service table, before dousing it with cream, hoping to cool it down, making it easier to ingest quickly. Just a dash of Sweet'N Low and it would be perfect.

Something about Sweet'N Low brought back good memories. The few good ones I had were typically at my pastor grandparents' house. My grandma was the perfect depiction of a housewife. A pastor's wife who specialized in making green bean casseroles and sun-soaked iced tea that would only be made perfect with a pink packet of Sweet'N Low.

Ah ... the taste of aspartame in the morning.

Don't ask me why I had two perfectly fit adults who took me in twice a year—for a week at Christmas and a week for vacation Bible school—to flaunt around church as tokens, before returning us in complete denial, turning a blind eye to our glaring dysfunction. I'd ask myself that question most of my life, never coming up with an answer that wasn't a complete and utter disappointment.

I got lost in thought as I sipped the warm heaven from the cup.

What had happened to my dad? He had always been such a hustler.

On the other hand, he had always been a schmoozer, user, loser too, but one that didn't struggle to have a stack of cash burning a hole in his jeans. He didn't follow the world's template for a "successful life" in the slightest. He had learned that cutting corners and taking risks typically ended up being worth said risk. He had to have money to support his drug habit, at the very least. I'm sure most of his "business plans" were brainstormed while fueled by a cocktail of crank and booze, however genius. Now he was just some sad, washed-up version of himself.

I guess it's true what they say. All money ain't good money.

My mind took me back as it typically did, but this memory—although completely illegal—was a fond one.

* * *

Hewlett-Packard Inc, Roseville, CA, November 1997

The crisp night bit at my nose, like a kid taking a chunk out of an apple. The smell of tall grass filled the air as we—my father, my sister and I—trampled it beneath our feet, trudging up a small hill, looking over the huge facility down below. We wore all black and my sister and I were jacked on Mountain Dew and Skittles, as was the typical lookout routine.

My dad had found a new hustle.

He had always been a sucker for a quick come up, which didn't exclude dumpster diving. Before he found this gold mine, he'd lurked behind grocery and department stores and the occasional upscale neighborhood. The day-old bread and defective sportswear he'd find there didn't come close to the spoils he would retrieve from this one.

This—was Hewlett-Packard.

Windows 95 was not only new on the tech scene but was exploding and Hewlett-Packard threw away a lot of crap. Perfectly working disks filled their dumpsters, along with laptops with damaged boxes and other swap-meet gold. My dad would rent a truck from the local rent-a-car, fill the bed with the "damaged goods," then peel off into the starry night, his two girls cuddled up together in the bench seat, passed out beside him.

My dad had cased the place for weeks before his first attempt, so he knew the ins and outs of the place and the only tricky thing would be getting past the roving security, that made rounds in increments of five to ten minutes. He would need a lookout.

The mix of not being the most sociable person, as well as incredibly cheap, left only one option for most of my dad's "business." He would have us kids do his dirty work. The same was for when he had his chimney sweep business and his window cleaning business. The older kids would flip through the white pages of the local phone book making cold calls. This was no different. The need for caffeine and sugar to keep us awake came from the optimal time for the haul being between four thirty and five in the morning. Shift change.

We hunkered down on our bellies, only our flush cheeks and starry eyes peeking over the hill through the grass, walkie-talkie in hand. My sister and I looked at each other with eyes wild with excitement. One thing about life with my dad was—good or bad—it was always an adventure.

In our minds we were real spies, with our black beanies and matching child-size gloves to bring it all together. The adrenaline pumped through our little veins, making us break out in giggle fits.

"HEY!" My dad's scorned whisper broke through the night. "QUIET! YOU'RE SPIES REMEMBER? SPIES DON'T MAKE A SOUND!"

We swallowed our excitement, nearly biting holes in our lips, trying to contain our laughter.

"Now, Jamie—You're on the radio—"

"Aw, but I wanna do—"

"Hush!" my dad cut me off quickly. "You have the important job, Kate. You tell Jamie when you see a guard. You're the lookout. It's the most important job; can you handle the most important job?"

I was eight, so obviously I bought the load of crap with a sure glee. I nodded dramatically.

"Good … alright, I'm going down. Jamie … What do you say if you see a guard?"

"Get down!" Jamie whispered.

"Yes, and say it quietly."

"OK!" Jamie's little whisper carried further than it should have, but maybe it was the excitement of it all amplifying each detail. With that, my dad made his way down the hill and over the high gate, slinking with the stealth of a cat burglar. He would return and make the trip again, until the sun rose high above us, blowing the safe cover of night, where he would point to the truck, indicating it was time to pack it in.

* * *

SHERATON GASLAMP DISTRICT HOTEL

"I'm posting an ad." Keith's voice broke me out of my daydream.

"No, the fuck you're not. I'm not ready yet."

"Well, get ready. The morning commuters are already at work; you're gonna miss the lunch clients."

"I'll get in the shower in a few minutes and when I'm ready, I'll let you know."

"Mm-hmm," was his irritated reply. I didn't care. I was enjoying my coffee and was not looking forward to the day of disassociation that lay ahead. I tapped my long acrylic nails on the coffee cup just to irritate him, making it known that I was taking my time. But not too long, I just wanted to fuck with him a little, not ruin the rest of the day with a real fight, that would ensue if I took it too far. I knew his limits of tolerance and I was skating within them. Barely. Microaggression was a well-crafted art form at this point in our relationship.

I sat with my legs crossed, propped up on the table for a moment longer before I stood slowly. My robe fell down into place, covering my cheeks. I paused and yawned, enjoying one last view of the city, before sauntering slowly to the bathroom.

I was barely rinsing the conditioner from my hair when Keith opened the door, getting caught in a cloud of steam. The scalding hot water made its way down each of my curves before spinning into the large drain at my feet, washing away all of my problems, if only for a moment.

"You got a client at the exit."

I flung open the fog-covered glass door with an instant flash of rage boiling hotter in my blood than any scalding shower.

"How?!"

"I've been talking to him on Humaniplex," Keith replied nonchalantly, with an air that said two can play this game. He knew I had to take the call.

Humaniplex was a social network that created a safe space for providers and clients, each having to be reviewed and verified as safe and not law enforcement before getting a verified account. If I flaked on clients—I would be banned from the site. I glared with the devil dancing in the blue flames that were my eyes.

"You're a grade-A piece of shit; you know that?"

Keith responded by taking two steps into the bathroom and setting my phone on the counter.

"I'm going to the car. Text me when you're done."

"I fucking hate you," I said through a somewhat bewildered yet psychotic laugh. I was sure my words stung but he shrugged it off casually, replying, "I'll be in the car," before walking out the door, leaving me with only my rage to carry out his wishes.

I rushed around the room in an attempt to make myself more presentable, but there was no time.

Guys like the fresh out of the shower look right?

I figured a naked girl, wearing only a towel to answer the door, wouldn't be the worst greeting he ever got and calmed a tad. The knock came, freezing me into place in a wince, scrunching my eyes closed and bringing my shoulders up to my neck, as was my general, visceral response to such knocks. I opened my eyes and shook it off. I couldn't keep him waiting. I answered the door, trying to hide my complete and utter irritation at his presence.

"Hey, babe! Come on in!"

He instantly lit up at the sight of me, a smile of approval falling over his face as he almost skipped into the large, bright room. He was a five-foot-ten Caucasian man, late twenties or early thirties at most. The shirt and tie gave away that he undoubtedly worked in some sort of office setting. I felt a twinge of pity for him. I turned tricks for a living, and to me, even that was better than spending fifty hours a week in some cubicell, with fluorescent lights beating down on me. Thanklessly struggling to make a quota, so I pay for the only human contact I had felt in months.

I often made up my own stories about the clients, in an attempt to humanize them as best as possible, but it was difficult being as desensitized as I was at this point.

He set a thick envelope on the desk and sat on the bed. I picked it up, feeling the weight of it in my palm and knowing there was at least twice my asking rate within the white folds and set it back down, giving him a sultry gaze.

"Did you give me a big tip?" I said flirtatiously, the sweet words oozing from my pink lips like glaze.

"I did," he replied, playing into the banter, "and I'm about to give you another."

Gross.

I had become a natural at hiding my reactions behind a smile. I lay down on the crisp white comforter and let the towel fall away from my delicate skin. His eyes drank me in.

In an instant, he was licking me in long strokes and not in the typical place a girl would find a mouth cared to roam. My ankles. My armpits. More of my armpits, leaving a snail trail of saliva behind each section he covered.

Is he a client or a fucking Labrador?! I thought to myself.

I was so utterly disgusted, I had to stop him. I tried to hide my repulsion, before stating the obvious. "I—this is a little much for me. Do you care if we do something else?" I said in a somewhat apologetic tone.

He twinged in embarrassment, looking taken aback.

"But—we discussed this in the messages."

Fucking Keith. I wanted to fillet him open with a katana. *Scumbucket piece of shit motherfucker.*

"The messages—right … I think I may have misunderstood. So sorry about that … I just … I want to make you happy … I just—"

His little soldier had gone from full attention to half-mast at my reaction and continued to shrink into a little pink worm, the longer the conversation continued. I knew I'd have to resurrect it with a quickness for this to not come back and bite me in a review forum.

"Why don't you let me take the lead." I motioned for him to lay down and went to work in a systemic fashion.

"Just relax—"

Fucking Keith. I could have at least read his reviews. There were a lot of weird requests and I never shamed, but some were out of my level of comfort. Especially when completely unexpected. Had I known a client was coming, I could've scoured the "Provider Only" forums by simply typing his username into a search bar. Surely a provider would have mentioned this experience, being that people typically don't enjoy being fully saturated in another's saliva.

The client struggled to get hard at first but soon relaxed and within five minutes, he was done. I walked him to the door, apologizing again, before closing it behind him and letting a frown settle upon my brow. I was livid. My gaze fell on the envelope sitting on the nightstand and I swept it up in my slender, manicured fingers. I sifted through the bills to get an idea of how much was there.

They felt thick. My stomach sank.

I pulled out the stack of bills, verifying my worst fear.

They're fake.

"FUUUCKKKKKK!" I screamed, taking my head into my hands and clinging the roots of my hair tightly. When I saw Keith, I was going to murder him. I ran over to the computer and checked the site, barely able to keep my shaking hands still long enough to type in my password.

I was in.

Messages.

Click. I pulled up his profile.

He was unverified.

"*MOTHERRFUCKERRRRRR!*" I screamed again, tears rushing down my face. I knew there was no way to chase him. It was a big hotel with many an exit. Surely, he was gone by now. Another faceless, white-collared-shirt-donning, Caucasian male, effortlessly blending into the crowds of San Diego's million-plus inhabitants.

I almost picked up the phone to call Keith, then thought of one better. I was going to the car. I had to hatch a plan. I was done. I was done with this life and I was done … with him. I was shaking in anger, riding the elevator down to the parking structure, where I knew he'd be sitting in *my* car, watching basketball—or even better, porn—on his phone. I flung the door open like the living breathing definition of the hulk, making it ricochet, slamming itself back into me with a force that knocked me into the passenger's seat. I threw the stack of counterfeit bills in his face with a smack.

"WHAT THE FUCK, YOU PSYCHO BITCH!"

"IT'S FAKE! IT'S FUCKING FAAAKEEEE!" I screamed in his face in a full-tilt rage episode.

"WHY DID YOU TAKE FAKE MONEY THEN!" His reply only fanned the flames blazing within me.

"IT WAS FUCKING HUMANIPLEX ! HE WAS UNVERIFIED, YOU FUCKING IDIOT! I JUST GOT RAPED BECAUSE OF YOU!"

"MAN, YOU DIDN'T GET RAPED; YOU JUST DIDN'T GET PAID. STOP BEING FUCKING DRAMATIC."

"OH YEAH? WHAT THE FUCK DO YOU THINK RAPE IS, YOU IGNORANT FUCK? IT'S BEING COERCED INTO SEX! THAT'S WHAT THIS WAS. I FUCKING HATE YOU. I FUCKING HATTTEE YOUUUUUU!"

I lost my mind. My fists pummeled him as if they were Thor's hammer. He threw his hands up in defense at first and then attempted to grab the fists that were flying at his face in an effort to restrain me. Normally, he overpowered me easily. But, the sheer hate that fueled me was relentless. He popped the door open and pushed himself out of the car, falling on his back and kicking the driver-side door shut, creating a barrier between himself and me.

I quickly locked the doors of the running car and hopped into the driver's seat. A look of disbelief crossed his face, accurately predicting my next move and he bounded to his feet and ran to the front of the car.

"YOU'RE NOT LEAVING ME HERE, KAY!"

I revved the engine in a vain attempt to frighten him. No luck. He knew I wouldn't run him over. I lurched the car forward slightly and he jumped on the hood, his fingers grasping the metal where it met the windshield. I could barely hear what he said next over the sound of my murderous thoughts, but I could read his lips.

"You're not leaving me here, Kay. You're not *fucking* leaving me. I'll kill myself if you leave me."

Suddenly, I felt like Alice, falling down the rabbit hole.

We're all mad here, didn't you know?

The words echoed in my mind and my vision spun as it closed in and out. I opened my eyes but still saw red. Then black. Then nothing at all.

Why did this feel so familiar?

Like a scene out of a movie. Was it déjà vu? Or, had I just imagined this scenario so many times at the beginning of our acquaintance that I knew how the story went in deep detail? It didn't feel as good as I'd hoped. I wanted to leave him, but every inch of my life as I knew it had him woven into the fabric. He set it up that way, I'm sure. As any narcissistic abuser would, for optimal control. My car. My apartment. His name was written on all of them. I couldn't leave. Not without leaving with nothing, and I wasn't prepared for that. I would have to have a better plan.

I watched him beg on the hood of the car for the better part of a half an hour, before I switched off the engine and popped the driver-side door.

"Thank you, babe—thank you—I knew you wouldn't—"

I cut him off, mid pathetic sentence, with a wave of my hand.

"Don't fucking touch me. Don't fucking talk to me. I'm getting my shit. And I'm going home. Once I'm there, I'm going somewhere to be alone. If you try to stop me. I'm not coming back."

"So you're just gonna leave me at the house with your dad?"

"I'll drop you at Mik's."

"Kay—"

"NOT—ANOTHER WORD!" I growled at him. "Not another—fucking—word!"

Chapter Thirteen

Best Western, Pismo Beach, CA, December 2009.

Taking in my father was a risk I know, but I couldn't bear to see him out in the cold. He had been a transient on and off for years. My worst fear was getting a phone call that he was dead. He'd go missing for long periods during my life and each time, I'd hold my breath waiting—just waiting for the inevitable call. Him living at my house was the only way I'd know he was safe at home—for the most part. At least that's what I thought until I tried to call him.

Typically, he'd answer my call on the first ring. But not this time. I got a sinking feeling in my stomach. My dad was a junkie and a thief through and through. Worst-case scenario, he had OD'd on the floor of my studio apartment. Best-case scenario—he had robbed me blind.

I hung up my phone in frustration, as the annoyingly robotic "you have reached 5-3-0" answering machine message came over the line, for the umpteenth time that morning. Joy did not fill me as I looked at a focused Keith, fully engaged in a preseason game on the television. I had to tell him and didn't want to deal with him on top of everything else I had swimming through my head. I went to raise my voice but paused. Was it really necessary to go back? To which my knowing replied a wholehearted yes.

"Keith?"

No response. He was glued.

"HEY! EARTH TO KEITH!"

"Huh?" An irritated confusion swept his face.

"We—We gotta go back."

"What? Why?"

"My dad's not answering the phone and I have a bad feeling."

Keith shook his head, processing for a moment before his expression changed, indicating the lightbulb above his head finally went off.

"The safe."

Of course he would think of the money first. I guess in all fairness he didn't have a lifetime of trauma dealing with my father's use and overdoses, but still.

"Yeah." The words came slowly, knowing the storm that would follow.

"Fuck, man, I told you this shit was a bad idea—"

"Hold the fuck up," I cut him off in an attempt at damage control. "We don't know anything yet, just—*chill!*"

Keith held it in, but I could see his head was spinning. We left the Pismo Beach hotel room in a flash, and drove the four hours up the 101, back home. The only words spoken between us were quick and to the point—hanging in the stale air like dry bread—bland and void of substance.

"At least I wrote a fire-ass song," I said, trying to remind him that the trip wasn't a total waste. He nodded in silence for a moment before responding.

"The song is fire … Franks gonna have a field day with this one." I smiled. He knew what he had. He was just dumb as a box of rocks in some very important departments. I often wondered what would have happened between us had we met in another place. In another time.

I probably would've run as far as humanly possible in the other direction.

Probably.

The song was "The Reason." A song I would go on to record and not only would it land me a management contract but would be the pioneering song for my career. It wouldn't make the radio or even get published but it was my foot in the door. I had a product. Proof of my talent and it would serve me well. But for now … I was suppressing a panic attack.

We pulled up to the complex and the car was barely in park before my door flung open and my feet pattered across the pavement, then up the case of stairs leading to my front door. I tried the knob. It was locked. I fumbled with my keys, my hands shaking, eventually coercing the door open. One look inside proved my father wasn't there. I was filled with relief, although my stomach sunk and my face twisted into a familiar frown, a deep line settling between my eyebrows.

That only left the other option.

I ran toward the dresser, pulled open the drawer, and unlocked the safe as quickly as possible. I could hear Keith's feet pounding their way up the stairs. I closed my eyes and took a deep breath before lifting the heavy lid. I almost couldn't look. I took another deep inhale and peeked from one eye. It was there. My body held on to the fear like an old familiar friend, even at the sight of the cash. I didn't trust him because he couldn't be trusted. I knew I had gotten lucky this time. My thoughts were swiftly interrupted.

"Is it gone?!" Keith's voice boomed from behind me, with a reserved panic.

I slumped over in relief. He ran over to the dresser and hovered over me, as I sunk deeper into my sprawled position.

"It's here."

"All of it?"

"Looks like … the locks not tampered with so … it's here."

Keith took two steps back and flopped down on the bed. Our relief filled the room before my anger canceled it out.

"WHERE THE FUCK IS HE?!"

I had good reason not to trust my dad. When I was eighteen and had sold my first $40,000 in structured settlement payments for $14,000, I was absconding parole. I was on my way to Georgia with my dad (where they didn't extradite juvenile parole cases) and just so happened to get pulled over in my hometown for a broken tail light. I was arrested on the spot. I gave my dad my card and pin number to put money on my books and he drained my account. Every. Fucking. Penny. I couldn't trust him around a pack of Tic Tacs, let alone everything I owned.

Just then the phone rang. It was him. I answered it in a fury.

"Where the fuck are you?! I've been calling you for hours! I thought you were dead or God knows what! I just drove all the way back from Pismo Beach because I couldn't get ahold of you!"

"Whoa sorry, kid … I fell asleep."

Code for nodded out.

"Fell asleep *where*?!" I demanded.

"At my friend's house."

Code for trap house.

"What the fuck, Dad. I just wasted a whole day and lost out on money cause you couldn't answer your fucking phone."

178

The amount of carefree in his tone was audacious and infuriating. I was sick of fixing things I didn't break and was realizing I was in over my head. I wanted to give up. But I couldn't, not just yet. The web I had woven had me tangled in its sticky threads and I was stuck with the option of putting up with his shit or putting him out on the cold hard streets of LA. Neither of which did I want.

"Sorry, man. I'm gonna crash here tonight, so I'll see you tomorrow."

Code for I'm too high to come back without you noticing, so I gotta level out a bit.

"Whatever."

I hung up the phone.

"Where he at?" Keith inquired.

"I don't fucking know. I'm gonna walk up to Subway and get a sandwich; you want something?"

"Nah, I'm good."

I pulled the single twenty-dollar bill from my wallet, returned with a six-inch tuna and placed the remaining sixteen back in the empty folds.

* * *

The next day would be one of the hardest emotionally I had seen in some time. With the shit storm I had managed to pull through unscathed in the last eighteen months or so—that was saying something.

I had to put my dad out.

I probably would've let him stay way past Keith's comfort, but he fucked himself out of his sweet deal by crossing one very hard line. He stole from me.

Driving back to the house after a day of running errands, I sat in the passenger seat, mentally preparing myself to deal with my child. I mean—

father. The dark cloud that had been following him around had expanded into every crack of my tiny apartment. I was convinced that his black hole of an auric field was the cause of my plants dying. You could argue that he forgot to water them. That would be a valid point. Except the one tiny negating detail that they were cacti. They rotted out from the roots.

I opened my wallet and realized a five-dollar bill was missing. A familiar frown covered my face.

"What's wrong?" Keith asked with concern.

"I had sixteen dollars in here," I replied as I leafed through the bills, hoping I had made an error.

"How much you got now?"

I looked up at him.

"Eleven."

"Your dad?" I shrugged my shoulders unsurprised but thoroughly heartbroken all the same.

"Had to have been."

"Least it was a five," he said with a disappointed shake of his head. I looked at him with a cocked eyebrow and blinked slowly, unamused.

"No, it's the principle." My words filled the car with a salty air.

"How you gonna prove it?" he rebutted, still focused forward.

"What do you mean? It's *proved*," I spouted back at him "I had sixteen dollars—now I have eleven. Simple math."

"It's not what you know, it's what you can prove, Kay." I had heard him utter this statement many times before and while that was true in a court of law, as he should know from the times I *knew* he was being unfaithful, it held no water when it came to me. I knew many things I couldn't prove and believed them all the same.

"That rule doesn't apply when they live in your house rent free," I shot back.

"True, true." Keith realized it best not to reason with the unreasonable and we drove back in silence. I spent the hour car ride in traffic, wondering how to best confront my dad. I was done. It was one thing to support him, give him my bed, feed him, clothe him and buy his cigarettes. It was quite another to lose peace due to not knowing if the TV or guitar was next. But, I wouldn't have to wonder for long because my dad was sitting on the stairs when I walked up.

"'Sup, kid?"

Keith passed him, walking directly into the apartment, without giving him so much as a look.

"Whoa?! What's his problem?" He played the role of the shocked and offended victim well.

Somebody get this guy an Oscar.

I gave him a once-over. It was now or never.

"Money is missing out of my purse, Dad." I was straight to it, bullshit never being my forte.

The words "it wasn't me" came as expected to which I was fully prepared.

"Oh yeah, who was it? You're the only one here and you were asking me for money before I left."

"How much is gone?" He was trying to set up his escape route. Minimization was his gift. He knew it wasn't a large sum and was hoping he could play that card. If only he had realized beforehand that said card was nonexistent in the deck of trust and respect.

"Five dollars."

"You wanna split hairs over five dollars?!" His feigned outrage made me sick to my stomach, which was currently eating a hole in itself.

"It's the *principle!*" I hissed through my teeth.

"Well I don't know what to tell you kid. I didn't take your five dollars." He laughed trying to lighten the mood.

Check the trash.

My intuition beckoned. I ignored it. Such a weird thing intuition. Always the most unexpected hunches. I stared in disbelief at the sad, slumped over, lump of a man on my stairwell.

Check the trash!

My intuition pushed again, this time a little louder. It was trash day. There was no trash. But, when my intuition spoke up a third time, I knew better than to ignore it. Signs always came to me in threes, like warning shots. If I ignored the first two, the third was always a heavy hitter with consequences, so I got use to paying attention. The safe was the first warning. This was the second. If I ignored it again, there would be a mess to clean up and I knew it deep within my soul.

I left him, casting one last disappointed look to where he sat on the stoop, before making my way toward the green waste bins that lined the back of the complex. I opened the first one. Empty. The second. Just my bathroom trash from earlier.

I went to close the lid when something glimmered, stopping me in my tracks. I looked closer.

Is that a beer can?

It was. Two actually. Two empty 211 cans, tucked away underneath the toilet paper rolls and Q-tips I had disposed of earlier that day. Nobody drank 211s; they were God awful. Except my dad. Those were his go-to. I snatched them up, with more disappointment than anger, and made my way back to the stairs. His eyes widened as I appeared in front of him, yielding the aluminum proof with a furrowed brow, but he quickly regained his composure, maintaining his star role of innocent character.

"What's that?"

"Just—don't, Dad." I could hardly look at him. I stood at the foot of the stairs, arms folded at my chest in defense, my lips pulled tight like a string purse. One quick read of my body language sent him over the edge. He knew I didn't believe him, but he'd take it to the grave, as was his way.

"THOSE AREN'T MINE, I SWEAR TO GOD, KID, I'M TELL-ING YA! THOSE—AREN'T—MINE!" Another drop added to the puddle of lies that rolled off his tongue like water.

"You can't stay here anymore, Dad. I can't trust you." My head fell and my stomach was twisted into knots. He had never protected me so why did it kill me inside that I couldn't protect him? But I knew—just like always—I had to protect myself first and while I couldn't save him from himself, I could either get out of the way of his path of destruction—or be left lying in its wake.

"So, what? You're just gonna kick me out on the street in the middle of the night?!" he exclaimed dramatically. The angle came right on time as expected. Every manipulation he tried to throw at me I swung at and hit out of the park.

I wasn't eight anymore. He couldn't talk me out of my birthday card money.

I was a grown up and his games were sad and old. I didn't take the bait.

"Nope … you can stay here tonight—but in the morning, you're on your own."

My dad's last resort for the win?

"Ever since the fire—" He went for it. Like clockwork. I cut him off cold.

"IT'S ALWAYS THE FIRE, DAD! IT'S FUCKED UP! YOU THINK I DON'T KNOW THAT? YOU THINK YOU'RE THE ONLY ONE WHO SUFFERED? YOU THINK YOU'RE THE ONLY ONE THAT CARRIES THAT TRAUMA WITH THEM EVERY DAY? NOOOOOO! BUT YOU'RE THE ONLY ONE WHO USES IT AS AN EXCUSE TO DO NOTHING BUT BEG AND MOOCH AND DESTROY EVERYONE AROUND YOU. IT'S LIKE YOU'VE GOT A REVERSE MIDAS TOUCH OR SOMETHING! EVERYTHING YOU LAY A FINGER ON TURNS TO SHIT AND IT'S YOUR DOING! YOU DO IT! AND EVERY TIME, YOUR EXCUSE IS THE SAME. THE FIRE. THE FIRE. IT WAS FIFTEEN YEARS AGO, DAD!. LIFE—WENT—ON!" I said the words but I didn't hear them. Like I was screaming into a void as I left my body and my consciousness was relocated to a different place in time.

* * *

THE BAYLESS APARTMENTS, RED BLUFF, CA, CHRISTMAS DAY 1995

It was Christmas Day and though snow never fell in the small Northern California town of Red Bluff, a bite hung in the air above the frost-lined grass, in respect of the holiday festivities. Up until this fateful day in December, the holidays always held an air of excitement for me.

My home life was far from the storybook picture one would hope for, but something about the lights and songs about reindeer made all of my troubles melt away like a soft mint on my tongue. I had an expectant glee that carried me like a cloud through the days that would precede the holiday and I fully intended on riding that cloud until some outside force knocked me back into the orbit of my harsh reality.

That force would come early this year and with a much heavier hand.

I was hyped on sugar cookies and in a full-blown argument with my older sister Niki when the troubles of the day began to unfold.

"HE IS TOO REAL!"

"IS NOT!"

"YES, HE IS! SANTA *IS* REAL!"

"*MOM!* TELL HER SANTA'S NOT REAL!"

My mom didn't even look up from the glass of homemade blackberry wine she was pouring.

"She can believe whatever she wants—but the bikes are from me."

My jaw dropped to my chest and my heart shattered into pieces at my feet. I ran out of the cluttered apartment and jumped on the new bike that lay sprawled in front of the door and rode off into the complex.

He isn't real. Santa isn't real.

A tear fell from the corner of my eye and quickly fell to my lips accelerated by the wind. I swallowed it into my mouth with a solemn and silent promise to myself that I wouldn't cry.

It's Christmas. Don't you know you're not supposed to cry on Christmas?

I shook off the incident and went to find some neighborhood kids to play with. We lived in a notoriously sketchy complex on the wrong side of the tracks, but it was home. It couldn't have been more than ten minutes since the whole Santa Claus debacle, when I was snapped out of my Christmas Day sugar rush by a loud whistle. It was my mom.

My ears perked at the sound like a sheep dog listening for wolves. The whistle ripped through the chilled air again. One thing I knew better than was to keep her waiting. You heard that whistle, you came running like the house was on fire. I pumped my little legs as hard as I could and screeched to a stop in front of my mother and two older sisters who were standing on the walk. They were crying. My head tilted to the side as I attempted to process just what had happened here and as I took it in fear flooded me.

My mom didn't cry. I don't think I had ever seen her cry. Not even once.

Until now.

"What ... what's a matter?" my little voice cracked leaving white clouds of breath in the air as I spoke.

"Leave your bike here and go to Angie's." The words came out cold as the air around them, lacking explanation. My feet stayed put.

"Now!" Her voice carried over me so loudly I could feel the sound wave penetrating my chest.

"But, what ...?" Emotions I couldn't name were bubbling up within me. My sisters tears ran flush.

"Go!" she boomed, her eyes flashing a brighter shade of green.

It wasn't a suggestion as I had once thought; it was a command. Angie was my babysitter who lived on the other side of the complex. I knew better than to challenge her. My chin touched my chest as I stomped away in the opposite direction and walked into Angie's house without a knock.

"My mom said to come here," I said with a pout, slamming the door shut behind me. The windows rattled as the door closed with a loud thud. Normally, this behavior would be labeled as "uncalled for" and I'd be sent to a room to think about what I'd done, but the punishment didn't come, which made it seem all the worse.

"I know, babe. Merry Christmas! Sit on the couch and watch TV. I'll make you a snack."

"OK," I pouted, collapsing on the plush grey loveseat. I was so confused and angry.

I want to play outside. Why can't I play? Why were they crying? Why wouldn't they tell me what was wrong?

I had so many questions, but I dared not ask. Although Angie seemed to save face, I could tell even she was shaken, being that her hands were. The news was on.

I hate the news. The news is boring.

I picked up the remote with the full intent of flipping through the channels until the screen displayed Cartoon Network. I guess being at Angie's wasn't so bad. I didn't mind taking advantage of the cable box I didn't have access to at home. I scanned the large remote for the right button, but before I could press it, I was stopped in my tracks. The news looked—familiar.

Wait. Why is my dad's house on the news?

I focused in on the reporter and as the words fell from her lips, I knew my life had changed forever.

"Tragedy struck the small town of Ukiah last night, as a fire ravaged this house around two o'clock, early this morning. Police say that the house had caught fire by what appeared to be a candle. The power was shut off earlier this week due to nonpayment. The mother, Christine Kuns, was able to escape the horrifying blaze, with two of her children, one a newborn, the other approximately ... ten years old. The other four children who lived in the home, were pronounced deceased this morning, due to smoke inhalation. They were all under seven years old ... the youngest ... being sixteen months. We will have more on this case at eleven o'clock, back to you in the studio."

My dad lit the candle.

He said he left to try his luck at the casino—you know—gamble the money they had so he could get the power turned back on. He left the candle in a macramé planter. The house was up in flames minutes after he left. They say the dry Christmas tree was an accelerant, but in my father's mind, it was him that was the "accelerant." No sober, straight-thinking human puts a candle in a macramé hanging planter. Not. One.

Four kids dead. They were just babies. He never came back from that. My dad's screams penetrated my disassociated state.

"Well now I can't stay here! I'm not staying with someone who's calling me a thief and a liar!"

I knew this play. He wanted money.

"Go, then! The gate's right there!" I half pointed to the exit, too exhausted to fully lift my arm.

"I don't have any money!"

"Yeah, that's where I thought this was going—"

"FUCKK YOUUUU, KATIIEEE!" His screams bounced back in echo against the quiet street.

"*Lower. Your fucking. Voice,*" I growled quietly, fully expecting to see my neighbors emerge from their doors, to see what all the commotion was about. They didn't.

"How much is it, Dad? What's your number this time?" I couldn't believe I was saying it, but it seemed like the only way out, as was typical with Emitte. He always had a price.

"I need at least forty dollars for a hotel room."

He wasn't gonna get a hotel room. He was gonna get dope.

"Babe!" I yelled up the stairs. A few moments passed with my dad and I exchanging death stares, before Keith popped his head through the screen door.

"Give him forty bucks."

"Nah, man—" he began to refuse, but I quickly canceled him.

"*Hey!*" My voice shook the still night surrounding us. "*I said*—give him forty bucks!"

Keith reached in his pocket, pulled out two twenty-dollar bills and tossed them with disgust at my father.

"That's what your relationship with your daughter is worth to you … right there." Tears filled my eyes but the sheer defiance I had likely inherited from him refused to blink, for chance that he could see them fall. He would prey on my weakness at the first sign, of which I showed none. I stood stoic before him, prepared for the worst.

"FUCK YOU, KATIE!" he snarled again.

"Hey, man!" Keith came through the door and took a few intimidating steps toward my father.

"Watch your fucking mouth! This girl done everything for you! You ain't gonna speak to her any type of way! Get—*your shit*—and get the fuck on!"

Emitte knew better than to try his luck. He gave me one last pitiful scowl before snatching up his backpack and disappearing into the night. I climbed the stairs slowly, all of my energy being used on keeping my calm. I lay my heavy body on the soft sheets … and fell asleep.

Chapter Fourteen

The streets were lined with palm trees, creating large black shadows, contrasting the dim glow of the streetlights that had just come on, flickering as they did. The sun had set and all the proof that was left of its presence was a sherbet sky, that swirled like the Thrifty's ice cream that colored in spaces of my childhood with pink and orange. A car alarm went off in the distance as a dog barked and I stood huddled by my car, attempting to ward off the cool of the Los Angeles night, by chain-smoking cigarettes.

I had forgotten my jacket again because … well … it's Los Angeles. Rarely was it cold enough to need one. You could typically find me in flip-flops if I was caught in the rain because I'd never seen it rain for more than an hour in this sunny Southern California paradise that I'd called home for the better part of the last two years. I was waiting for Frank.

The small part of me that was aware of my current reality and its surroundings noticed a large black SUV pull in the empty lot with a lurch and zoom forward into a parking space.

OK, Mario Andretti, I thought to myself. It had to be him. I flicked the cigarette across the asphalt and it landed with a small firework of spark as the red glow faded from sight. The man hopped out of the vehicle with an undeniable cool. He was dressed casually, but as he walked toward me, he had the strut of a GQ runway model. Well—if GQ models were five feet nine. Confidence was surely not a problem for him. I had met him in a corner store parking lot in Inglewood, but I've always said that the best stories begin in the most peculiar of places. He and Keith went way back.

* * *

THREE MONTHS EARLIER

We had stopped to grab a few swishers at a Korean-run liquor mart when the fated reunion of schoolyard playmates took place. The conversation quickly turned from the typical family talk, to me.

Keith demanded I sing.

"*Here?*" I asked in disbelief.

"Yeah, lil' mama, let me see what you got in your arsenal." Frank's green eyes flashed with charisma. I took a moment and then belted my heart out for the world to hear. Well, maybe not the world, but my voice surely carried over three square blocks. I finished to a round of strange, liquor store patrons' applause. A small crowd had formed unbeknown to me. Small, meaning the two gentlemen who were exiting the store stopped short of their cars to hear the performance.

"White girl got soul!" a kind old man shouted in our direction, as he climbed into his Buick LaSabre. I looked at Frank, whose eyes registered with a flash of dollar signs, before he broke the silence.

"You got anything recorded?" he asked with a tilt of his head, obviously calculating things I couldn't quite discern in his mind.

"Na-uh," I replied, looking at Keith. The ear-to-ear grin on his face confirming, what I already knew. I killed it.

"No contract, nothing?" he asked almost suspiciously.

"No, I'm ... yeah—just getting my feet wet," I said with a laugh.

"Just getting your feet wet? Shit," he replied with a laugh. "If you can do in the studio what you just did here, you gone be a whole-ass ocean—ya heard me?!" I smiled, almost embarrassed. I never did know how to take a compliment.

"You wrote that? Or that's somebody else's?" Each question dug deeper, but I didn't mind. I could tell this was no vain interest.

He sees it. He sees what I believe in. Why I do all this; why I try so hard.

He believed in me more than I did, I think and I had just met the man. Like some fated spell had fallen over him and something clicked into place, completing a cosmic equation that until this moment had been nothing but a jumbled mess of dark matter and meteors.

Like the moment of the Big Bang. But, only in my universe. I felt a knowing deep, deep within my core. This was something.

"Yes!" I quickly replied. "I have a ton of them."

Frank and Keith looked at each other for what seemed like forever, before laughing and shaking hands.

"Alright—let's see what she can do. I'ma get you some tracks."

"Sounds good, man," Keith replied for me.

* * *

Now I was holding myself together with nicotine and prayers as he walked in my direction.

"Keta Kay!" he shouted excitedly as he approached.

"Hey, man, how you doing?" I embraced him in a quick hug, my shivers quite visible at this point.

"Girl, you part Eskimo or what? Standing outside in the freezing cold like an icicle. Come on, chatterbox, let's get you inside to defrost."

"If you'd have driven here like you skirted into that parking space, I wouldn't have been standing here freezing my tail off Daytona No Hundred."

We chuckled and our witty banter filled the air as we made it into the studio and down the hall to the lab.

"Keta, this is Ran—Ran, Keta." It was a fairly informal introduction as Ran was deeply focused on a large board and screen doing masterful things I would be awed by later in the night. He threw a wave in the air but didn't look up.

"You ready?" Frank looked at me expectantly.

"Now?!" I was shocked at his eagerness, but figured he had the right idea. The longer I stood there, the longer my nerves had to spiral.

Jump headfirst for best results, that's my motto.

"You got it memorized right?" Ran asked, looking at me for the first time.

"Her memory like a computer, bro," Frank bragged on my behalf. I smiled, feeling a wave of love and support. We were strangers, but I felt like I was home.

I walked into the huge soundproof booth that was a beautiful, stained oak with clear glass windows and let the heavy door shut softly behind me. I could see Frank talking, but I couldn't hear him through the glass. He pointed to the stand and, as if in a game of charades, put on an invisible pair of headphones. It clicked. I reached for the headphones and fit them snuggly on my ears with the biggest smile my face had ever seen. It was like they were made for me.

"I feel like a fuckin' Verizon wireless commercial!" I heard Frank laugh over the headphones.

"CAN YOU HEAR ME NOW!"

"Yes, Frank. I can hear you." My smile bled through the words.

"Alright, Miss Kay, we gonna take you from the top. Just give us a full run so you could get acclimated to the mic and get your levels. Then—our resident genius Ran here—will walk you through it. Capisce?"

I partially understood. Studio lingo was a foreign language, but I could deduce with the best of them.

"Hit it from the top and sing it all the way through. Got it?"

I took in a deep gulp of air and nodded.

"Alright—*let's go!*" Frank clapped his hands loudly with unwavering enthusiasm. The music came over the headphones and I closed my eyes and took another deep breath.

It's just like singing in your room. No different. Just sing your little heart out. You got this.

My self-talk was abruptly interrupted by a voice in my headphones. It was Ran.

"You—that was where you come in." His dry tone was deafening. I watched him look at Frank with an air of mild irritation. It was a rookie mistake, sure. But I didn't miss it. I was talking myself off a ledge in my head.

"I—um—" I stuttered in the mic.

"What's up, Kay? What you need?" Frank asked, trying to hide his concern.

"I just—can I turn off the lights?"

"Um—yeah … there's a dimmer by the door. See it?"

"Yeah, I got it." I flipped the dimmer all the way down and disappeared from sight.

Ah … much better.

"We gonna run it one mo' again—you ready?"

"Ready."

The music filled the speakers and this time, I didn't hesitate. It was just me and the music. Just as it had always been. From the first perfect syllable, I lost myself in the lyrics and let the ballad tear me to pieces and build me back again. I felt the room grow thick with emotion, like fire coursing through my veins. I swam in the beautiful sound that was mine and mine alone. That magical something that carried me through every step leading me to this moment was very much here within me. Chills ripped through my flesh as I hit the final note coming back into my body. I opened my eyes.

The track stopped.

I was breathing heavily and a tear fell from the corner of my eye. I looked out the glass to two grown men staring at each other wide-eyed in awe.

"Did I—I mean—was that—good?" I asked hesitantly. Frank leaned in to press down the button on the intercom.

"You telling me you never done this before?" he asked with a cock of his head.

"Nope ... first time," I replied through a nervous chuckle.

"*Well, shit!*" Frank replied almost dumbfounded. He looked at Ran, who now wore a smile, nodding his head at a desk that resembled the motherboard of a spaceship, before saying the most beautiful words I'd ever heard.

"Alright then ... Let's run it again."

* * *

I drove home in a daze, the blur of traffic at a slow crawl on the 101 south, red glaring tail lights soaking into my retinas, only further distorting my vision. I don't know how long it took me to get home, but I knew I had smoked four cigarettes, one after another, in rapid succession.

I was now parked on a pitch-black street, blocks away from my house, sitting in a still-running car, staring blindly ahead. This was supposed to feel good, yet here I was, gripping the steering wheel, as if to let go meant my lungs would collapse into themselves, once and for all.

I was no stranger to panic attacks, anxiety was an old friend, and though lately it only visited about as much as a distant relative on holiday, it was here now taking my breath away. Reminding me what it felt like to be alive by taking the one thing I need to stay that way. Such irony. I wasn't allowed to feel good. It was always a trick. Didn't I know that by now?

If it feels good, they have something to take from you.

If it feels good—now you have something to lose.

The cherry of the cigarette that I held between shaky fingers had burned down to the filter and fell to my leg. I watched it burn on my jean, feeling the sharp heat eating its way through my protective layer. I wanted it to burn.

Remind me what it feels like to be alive. Pain. Sweet pain.

Tell me your secrets and I'll tell you mine.

The scorching sting registered mere moments later and I knocked it off of my leg with a quick burst, dispersing the vibrant sparks. I winced—although barely—before tracing the hole in the singed jean with my fingertip, letting the fray dance as I passed over it again and again. I fingered the hole, ripping it open to expose the soft skin that lay beneath. Skin. Such a funny thing. I was sure it was a novelty at best. Couldn't protect from any real danger, that was for certain.

We're all just underbelly and arrogance.

Mine felt like the inside of a rose. I related to a rose on so many levels. I understood why it lined its stem with thorns, being so beautiful you needed some sort of deterrent. Without my thorns, it would be even easier for someone to steal me from myself. Rip me up from my roots, cut me down to size, put me on display until my petals wilted and death became me, discarding me, never once stopping to smell my sweet fragrance. I needed these thorns. Even if I pricked myself from time to time.

My phone rang, filling the car and my head with all too much sound. I picked it up to see the name Mom written across the screen. I almost answered but thought twice of it.

Not now. I don't have the energy in me to pretend now.

I leaned my head on the window and was taken away by a familiar memory. One I had tried so hard to forget.

* * *

RED BLUFF, CA, JANUARY 2002

A peculiar placid silence held the night with the exception of the patter of my bare feet on the asphalt and the deafening sound of my heart crumbling into gravel-sized chunks. I knew this long stretch of backroad like an old church hymn, straight for two miles until you hit the fork. A right would take you nowhere and a left would take you into the small dirt town that held the secrets of its evil deeds in its bowel.

Everyone had a secret here; you could see it in the dead of their eyes. If they pretended it never happened long enough—maybe it didn't.

Who's to say what happened and not? Who's gonna prove it?

Tell the truth they said … I'll tell them you're a liar.

My word against yours and who the hell is gonna believe you?

They say the land was cursed. Legend woven into the fabric of the small town's history. The last hanging county in the west was built on top of a native burial ground. Pure sacrilege. Now, it was the home of meth labs and trailer parks, housing dope-fiend welfare recipients for miles. Everybody was poor. Even the people not considered poor were poor. They just didn't have to wait in line begging for day-old bread or government cheese that melted like plastic and tasted not much different.

My foot had started to bleed from a cut I didn't have time to inspect. Could've been anything, glass or sharp rock. It didn't matter though. Add it to the list of things going wrong on this fine Tuesday evening.

Wet'n'Wild mascara painted black lines into my cheeks like a Viking going to battle. I was anything but. I was a thirteen-year-old child running—running fast and far—from the owner of the voice in my head, still screaming, though I had surely put a mile of distance between us now.

"I'm gonna put you out of your fucking misery!"

I ran for what seemed like hours until I found myself in front of a door. A door that I wished was mine. A home where I was wanted. Tears blurred my vision as I lifted my dirty hand to knock. Spaghetti sauce covered my clothes and was caked into my tangled, wild locks. I was sure there was a chunk missing. Had to have been. Hair isn't strong enough to withstand being thrown through the air by it.

I knocked.

My favorite face in the whole world answered with a smile that was quickly replaced by a look of sheer horror.

"Katie! What happened! Oh my God! Mooommm!" she screamed. "Mooommm!"

Linda darted to the door at the sound of her daughter's distress. Her eyes widened and a protective rage flooded over her.

"WHAT IN THE GODDAMN FUCK! I'M DONE! I'M CALLING THE FUCKING COPS. THIS SHIT CAN'T KEEP HAPPENING!"

"NOOOO!" I pleaded. "PLEASE DON'T CALL THE COPS! I'LL GET IN TROUBLE, PLEASE!"

I was heaving and hyperventilating at the same time. Not a fun combination of involuntary bodily functions. Alyssa rubbed my back and tried to calm me as Linda screamed into the receiver of the phone in the kitchen. I watched it all play out in slow motion like a highlight reel, except this wasn't ESPN, even if surviving the homes I frequented lately would qualify as an extreme sport. I tried to catch my breath, but it outran me by miles.

"What a fucking piece of work!" Lynn muttered beneath her breath, expressing her infuriated disbelief, as she emerged from the kitchen with the wireless gripped tightly in her hand. Her knuckles were white and had she squeezed any harder, the phone might've turned to dust in her palms.

"They already reported you as a runaway—" Her top lip quivered as she uttered those reluctant words. "The cops are on their way."

"Nooooo!" came our unison scream, clutching each other tighter.

"They're gonna make her go back, Mom! Are they gonna make her go back?!" Alyssa asked her mother, her eyes welling over.

My mind replayed the event over again in my mind.

"You're in jail now. You get hungry; you get bread and water. That's what they feed you in jail."

The horrible voice trailed off and Linda's comforting one replaced it, bringing me back.

"I don't know, honey. I'm gonna try and talk to them when they get here but—" Linda had sat beside us and scooped us both up in her grasp before finishing her sentence. "—I don't know."

They were at the front door in under five minutes—small town and what have you. They tightened the cuffs to the last click, cutting off the circulation in my tiny wrists, before guiding me into the back of the cop car, one hand on the top of my head.

I couldn't hear through the glass my forehead was pressed against, but I stared into the front yard imagining magic words floating out of Linda's lips. The ones that would make officer Podunk nod his head in agreement and free me from my shackles, apologizing profusely for the misunderstanding. Impossible daydreams were how I soothed myself in such traumatic events. As common as they were, I had developed multiple methods of dissociation, this being the most effective by far.

I watched Linda as she raged in the front yard, feet away from the patrol unit, as the officer scribbled in his handy-dandy notebook, without looking down.

Hope fell away from me.

He didn't care. It was all a show to pacify her. Just another protocol. I was just another check on the list he needed to complete so he could go home.

"They already reported you as a runaway."

The words spun round on repeat, like a broken record in my mind. Can't deny it was a smart move. Gave them plausible deniability. Genius, actually. No matter how thin the line they were walking between that and insanity. The plan was going off without a hitch for the most part. I don't think they counted on my advocating for myself, knowing I had no one else to, because *they* were supposed to. It was almost the perfect crime.

What do you do when the people who were supposed to advocate for you are the ones causing you harm?

"I'm getting my gun and I'm gonna put you out of your misery!"

How do you say that to a child?

I prayed for a stroke, or an embolism, or some other fancy, brain-stopping disease so I could finally shut my mind off. We pulled into the mental health facility across the street from the juvenile hall.

What are we doing here?

I repeated my thought aloud this time, hoping for an answer.

"What are we doing here?" I asked with a clear, calm tone. The adrenaline had run dry and a familiar numb had settled in its place.

"They want you under psychiatric observation," the officer replied matter of factly, as he opened my door and gestured me out of the car.

They made it seem like I was crazy. Cheap shot, even for them. I guess that would be the only lie of an explanation that would make sense.

I was escorted through the halls and into another cold, sterile, nearly empty room where I was uncuffed and asked to sit down in a dirty, scuffed-up, plastic lawn chair. A woman sat across from me, as the officer closed the door behind him.

I peeled the hair caked in tomato sauce from the side of my face and tucked it behind my ear, as she began with the questions. None of them were new. I'd been asked these questions so many times I'd all but memorized the answers. I cut her off.

"I'm not suicidal. Never have been. Why am I here?"

Now to the reasonable person, these would seem like reasonable questions, but in this instance they were but an annoyance and the woman made it known.

"Let's just get through these questions. I don't want to be here all night."

Yeah, me either, lady.

I obliged. When she had written down my last answer, she sat rifling through the papers, making notes as I sat in silence, brushing stray tears from my lash line with my knuckle before they could accumulate enough to fall. The woman looked up from the file.

"Well, we're going to keep you for seventy-two hours on a 51/50 hold for observation, but I don't see why you wouldn't be released after the observation period is up." She used her scrawny, wrinkled index to push her glasses back up onto the bridge of her nose.

"I'm not crazy." I glared a hole through her at the mention of 51/50.

"Nobody said you were crazy, we just—" I interrupted her, my voice increasing an octave.

"That's what 51/50 means. I'm not crazy and I'm not stupid." The woman had started to get up.

"No, you're definitely not stupid, now let's just—"

"Where are you putting me?"

"What?" The look of confusion on my face mirrored in hers now.

"After the hold. Where am I going?"

She looked at the chart. "You'll be going back to—"

"NO!" My voice shook as I raised it, but I didn't back down.

"What do you mean *no*?" She didn't get it.

Even seeing me like this, shoeless, hair ripped out and covered in Italian food. She didn't get it. I shook my head in disgust and disappointment.

"What do you mean, no?" She repeated herself. "The plan here states—"

"I'm not safe there, don't you get that?!" I tried. I tried to keep my cool, but the thought of ever going back there struck a nerve I didn't know how to control. I took a deep breath, locking eyes with the strange woman who would decide my fate by signing on a dotted line, without a second thought.

"I'm not safe there—and if something worse happens to me—just know my blood is on your hands."

The first look of concern I'd seen cross her face all night, showed up just in time.

Well what do you know? There is a human in there.

She looked down at her papers.

"Katie, I'm going to ask you this one last time. Do you plan to hurt yourself?" I couldn't help but be infuriated by the idiocy of the woman. I laughed a single "ha" out of pure shock.

"Man, you're dim! *No!* No, please write that down—in the notes. Write down that if something happens to me, I had *no* plan to hurt myself and I would *never* hurt myself. I would like that documented please." I looked at her looking at me and gestured to the file sitting on the table.

"I don't see you writing."

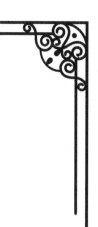

Chapter Fifteen

North Berendo St, Hollywood, CA, July 2010

A few months had passed and we had moved out of the sardine can into an actual apartment with rooms. It was beautiful. French bedroom doors, hardwood floors and large windows that lit up the open floor plan with natural light. I had never decorated anywhere I had lived before. Not since I was a kid anyways. You learn, after never being in one place longer than six months, that it's best to keep things ready to go at a moment's notice.

For the first time in my life, I was picking out bookshelves and curtains. My kitchen had matching silverware and dishes. I had never had matching anything before. Most of the houses I'd lived in used jelly jars as cups and Imperial Margarine tubs as Tupperware, so matching dishes was a pretty big deal for me.

We had gotten a packet from Ogilvy and Mather with contracts naming us principal performers in the commercial we had been dragged off Hollywood Boulevard to star in one random Tuesday evening, and while I thought it was cool to be in a commercial, I didn't expect it to be life-changing. I was wrong.

* * *

205

"Babe—"

I was asleep and hated to be woken up. The sun shone blindingly through the open French door where Keith stood holding two envelopes in his hand. Normally, I would have chewed him out for waking me from my beloved slumber, but the look on his face alone commanded my attention. I shielded my face from the intruding sun, dancing in my half-opened eyes.

"What?!" I groaned, clearly not amused.

"Look," he said with a quiet shock, handing me the envelopes. I opened them and pulled out the contents. There were ten checks in each envelope ranging from $500 to $1,000 each. I held the checks in my hand, blinking in disbelief. Half asleep, I wondered if I was dreaming.

"Is this real?" I asked, with a mix of dumbfounded awe.

"They look real—shit—real pretty."

"Says 'Mr. I don't want to go, I haven't shaved'?"

My impression of him didn't impress him at all.

"Hush ya mouth."

I laughed.

"Mm-hmm … Next time, I don't wanna hear nothing."

"Yeah, yeah …"

He almost didn't go.

* * *

HOLLYWOOD BLVD, HOLLYWOOD, CA, SEPTEMBER 2009

I had just taken my dad in and we had gone to grab dinner at our favorite restaurant. Famous Popeye's Chicken on Hollywood Boulevard. OK, it wasn't much of a restaurant, but I loved the shrimp po'boys, so to me it was fine cuisine. We had made our way to the entrance, where a long line drifted through it and slightly around the corner, which was typical of this location.

"Fuck!" I said with a start, stopping in my tracks.

"What?" Keith said over his shoulder, continuing forward on his mission for a three-piece.

A breast and two wings. White meat only. He always ordered the same thing and not just here, but everywhere. He was a man of habit. Didn't much like change.

"I forgot to put change in the meter." Keith looked back at the line that was still growing and then looked back at me.

"You want me to do it?"

"Nah, I got it," I said with a shake of my head, turning on my heels.

"I'll walk with ya," he called from behind. I looked over my shoulder to flash him a grin and yelling out in a sarcastic tone, "Aww, such a romantic."

"Shut up," he said with a huge smile.

Parking enforcement was no joke in Hollywood. I speed-walked back, leaving Keith in the lurch, half expecting their spidey senses to have picked up on my error. It was as if they could teleport tickets onto windshields. They were that quick.

I breathed a sigh of relief as I leaned over the curb to get a full view of my windshield wipers.

No ticket.

I dropped four quarters in the meter and as the last one deposited with a tink, I noticed two gentlemen staring at me. I got stared at a lot, so typically I didn't pay it any mind—but their energy was invading my field heavily. I almost asked them what they were looking at, when I noticed a video camera in their hand.

It was curious—but not odd. It was Hollywood. It's hard to see anything as odd in Hollywood. Between celebrity sightings, homeless people shitting in the alleys in broad daylight and everything between, you became pretty desensitized. I was still thinking, one brow cocked high, when the two men approached me. Keith was three steps behind them, distracted by his phone, as was typical.

"Hi! My name is James—this is Brandon!" He pointed to the other man. "We're street casting for a Yahoo commercial up the street and we think you'd be perfect!" They were dressed like the Ralph Lauren full-page ads I had flipped past in my *Cosmopolitan* magazines.

"*Me?*" I replied not able to curb my surprise. The first man did all the talking and left little room for space in between my words and his.

"Yeah so—it's their new 'It's you!' campaign—and the director wants real people to really drive it home. We're bringing in a bunch of people and start shooting in two hours. It's a ton of fun and if you don't make the cut, then we'll pay you two hundred dollars for showing up and if you do make it—you could potentially make a nice chunk of change." Both men wore huge smiles and seemed generally honest and harmless. I took the bait.

"It's *tonight?*"

"Yep! In two hours."

I thought for a brief moment before replying.

"OK, what do I have to do?"

The men beamed at my response.

How long had they been out here?

The answer to my question came, quickly ending my train of thought.

"Just look into the camera right here and—with the same bubbly personality you've had talking to us here—state your name and your phone number. If the director likes you, we'll call you in about forty-five minutes." Sounded simple enough.

I oozed personality as I focused in on the lens.

"OK—Hi! My name is …" I said my lines with a huge smile, an extra bit of sass and threw in a wink at the end, for good measure. I could tell I did a good job when the two strangers raised their brows in excitement before saying, "That was—A-Mazing!"

Just then Keith walked up.

God he's oblivious, I thought to myself with a hint of irritation. Please don't fuck this up.

"Hey, what's going on?" His voice came from behind and the two men turned in surprise at his presence. I answered quickly, as to not let minds wander too long.

"They're street casting for a commercial tonight!"

Keith looked suspicious as they gave their spiel again, adding, "You would be perfect too!"

Keith took it in, his smile growing wider as they explained, rubbing his palms together like an evil scientist.

"OK, OK, my name is Keith—"

We finished the recording, shook their hands and made our way back to Popeye's. I didn't expect to get the return call, but sure enough, I had barely finished my sandwich when the phone rang, requesting Keith and me to set on Hollywood and Gower.

Keith fought with me for fifteen minutes as I freshened up. I eventually won the argument by boldly stating the obvious.

"You haven't brought *a single fucking dime* in since I've known you. If these people wanna pay you two hundred dollars to show up to say Yahoo and eat dinner, you're FUCKING—GOIINNNGG!"

Now we were about $14,000 richer.

North Berendo St, Hollywood, CA, July 2010

My mind swam as I attempted to take it all in. These were only the first checks. There would probably be more. This was it. This was the chance I had been waiting for. I was done selling my body. Well, the whole thing at least. I instantly thought of a way out. My whole future flashed before my eyes and I knew I had just leveled up. This was my way out.

"I'm not hoing anymore, Keith," I said, quietly looking at the stack of checks still in my hand.

He didn't reply.

"Keith—"

"I heard what you said; I just don't think you heard what you said."

Anger boiled within me, but I took the mental pot off of the stove to keep from bubbling over. Compartmentalization at its finest, and I—was a pro.

"That doesn't even fucking make sense," came my exasperated reply. He was quick to respond as usual. Always talking—but not saying shit.

"No, what you said don't make sense. If it don't make dollars—it don't make sense. You got a fucking ATM between your legs. You'd be a fool to not withdraw." I hated how nonchalantly he was able to say those words. As if it was easy as selling pie.

"And you'd be a fool not to see the bigger opportunity here. Either way, I'm done. You don't have to see my vision; I'm done."

This subject didn't just come up out of thin air. I had brought it up a few times before and it had been shot down. Somewhere along the way, I realized that Glenda the Good Witch was right.

I *did* have the power all along.

A shift had happened. Keith wasn't running the show anymore. He pushed and fought me sometimes, but for the most part what I said went. This was no different.

I was Dorothy, but he wasn't Oz … He was just the little man behind the curtain. Any power he had, I gave him. The same was true with money and I was getting tired of carrying the load alone. Had he not been the reason I had connected with my now manager, proving somewhat useful, I would've been out the door. Or at least that's what I told myself and all hearts eat lies when they're hungry.

"So what are we gonna do for money?"

"Um … HELLOOO—EARTH TO KEITH," I said, waving the checks in the air.

"MORE OF THESE AIN'T A SURE THING!"

"THAT'S NOT MY ONLY PLAN, WISE GUY!" Our yelling filled the room before we each took a breath and lowered our tones, knowing we could either scream over one another, or—we could listen. The latter proved to be preferable, typically.

"Cool—I'm all ears. Lay it out for me, Pinky."

"It's the brain, stupid."

"Nah—you actin real pinky right now."

"Says the guy with no aspirations or other means of income. Don't start with me, I'm gonna hurt your feelings." My words stung like salt in an open wound. Cleansing for me, painful for him.

"What's your big plan, Kay?!" he said, his irritation showing in his body language as well as his tone.

"I'm gonna dance."

"Like strip?"

"Yeah," I replied, interrupting his disrespectfully amused chuckles.

"Ain't no money in that."

"You're hella dumb for saying that." I waved him off. I should've just done it, instead of trying to reason with an unreasonable man. He couldn't stop me anyways. I was one foot out the door, I just—I couldn't figure out how to move the other foot. It was as if it had been bolted in place. Some voodoo mystery. I could hear my sister's voice in the back of my head. *"I don't understand ... you're the most 'middle fingers to the world' girl on the planet. You do what you want, when you want, how you want. You've always been that way, Kate. Except when it comes to him. I just ... I don't get it."*

"It's not as much." His voice dropped me back into reality.

"We spend six grand on hotels and travel a month, so what I lose in profit, I make up for in overhead."

"You really thought this through, huh?"

"Yeah," I said, praying for the conversation's end. Bitter words hung on my tongue but I bit them down. They would fall flat and I knew it. It just wasn't worth the energy.

"You forgot one thing, Kay—YOU CAN'T DANCE!"

How the fuck did he know? I said the words in my head before quickly reminding myself to repeat those same words out loud.

"You don't know I can't dance. I've never even tried. Everybody learned somehow. I'm no different."

"You just gonna walk up in the club and try out with no experience." The gall of this man. I was disgusted and tired and tired and disgusted. What the fuck was so hard to comprehend?

I felt like I was explaining physics to a five-year-old.

212

I took in a deep breath and sighed.

I carefully constructed my next sentence, as not to leave any room for misinterpretation.

"No … I'm gonna buy a pole and take a class or something and then go. These checks give me a little bit of flex. I can take a few weeks to get a little more fluent with the art."

"You can't learn to pole dance in two weeks. That shit takes years."

Yeah, and if this conversation doesn't end, you're gonna meet an early grave.

I didn't say it. It just felt good to think it.

"Oh yeah, we'll see!"

"Alright, bet. We make a deal."

"I'm not making a deal. I'm done." I rolled back over and pulled up my blankets to my chin.

The day started with such promise and here he goes, just born to fuck shit up.

"No, hear me out. You get hired at a club in a month and you won't hear another word from me."

I coached myself mentally, as I often did.

Just agree so he'll leave you the fuck alone.

I flipped back over in the covers to face him again.

"Oh ye of little faith. Dumb bet. You got it."

I knew if I didn't get hired, I still wasn't going back to the old way, but he didn't have to know that. This would shut him up for now. We'd get to that bridge when we crossed it. Keith slid his palm across mine, ending in a snap and he had almost made his way out the door when I broke the second piece of news.

213

"Hey!"

"What?"

"And I'm going back to school."

Damn. I scolded myself. You couldn't just leave well enough alone. You know this shits gonna drag on now. I shook the thoughts from my head, knowing better to get it over with now.

"What school?"

"The Musicians Institute."

"Girl—do you know how expensive that school is?!" Keith scoffed at the idea. As if the mere thought was so preposterous, I ought to receive an award for audacity.

"I'll get grants and loans. I was in foster care; they gotta have something for me." Keith thought, leaning his tall, lanky, yet muscular body against the French door for a moment, before replying.

"You're really serious?" A look of surrender crossed his face. I didn't expect it so soon.

"As a heart attack. This shit ain't gonna be for no reason. The game was supposed to be the vehicle, not the destination. This train is moving forward and either you hop your ass on a boxcar or you're gonna get left behind."

Saying the left behind part was a risk, but I knew it had about an 80 percent efficacy rate of driving my point home. Keith made me promise frequently that I wouldn't leave him and though I often wanted to—I doubted I could. The trauma bond was strong and I had worked really hard to reform this low-down, dirty pimp into some resemblance of a partner. I didn't want the next girl in line to benefit from all of my struggle. Sick, I know, but that's where I was at. Couldn't have helped it if I wanted to.

"You tryna square up?"

"Pretty much," I said through a sigh.

The game had to wear on Keith too. Nobody wants that. You might think you do, but at the end of the day, nobody ends up in the game for any other reason than survival. People with options don't typically pick an occupation of underworld, carrying a minimum sentence of five years if you got caught.

Keith grew up in the jungles off of MLK. Not the best area. His parents and siblings who weren't incarcerated still lived there. He had already beat one pimping case. One of his brothers was doing life for murder and the other was doing a dime upstate on a feds' case. The system wasn't kind to black men. Shit, the system wasn't kind to me ... a Podunk white girl. I knew this was the only way this could work. My pain and trauma would not be in vain. His lips pursed out and down as he nodded his head.

"OK, Kay ... we'll try it."

* * *

HOLLYWOOD, CA, OCTOBER 2010

The next few months were the best months of my life. I could see it all coming together in a way I had only dreamed about before. Many a fantasy while lying on my bunk, counting that particularly sterile shade of off-white bricks in my cell, were spent envisioning a future that much resembled the one I was currently realizing. Of course, no one could ever imagine, or even want to for that matter, the way that it all came about, but that didn't matter now. It was behind me and I was a master at repression at this stage in my life.

I had made a dent in the dream I so desperately clung to. Before that fateful day where I sat on the bed in awe, staring at a stack of unexpected favor in check form, I almost had accepted my fate. My mind beat me down daily.

Just give up; it's never gonna happen.

I was defiant by nature though. The more that thought antagonized, the more I dug my heels in. I was going to make it out of here and when I did—I was taking all of these secrets to the grave.

I put on a mask and showed up as the girl I expected I would've been had I not experienced the tragedies that were my first two decades of relentless life. I thought I could fake it until I made it. If only it were that easy.

I had no idea what I was in for.

My mental health was the best it had been in years. I quit doing coke and stuck to my daily gram of weed consumption and alcohol from time to time, but I was in school now, so I had to show up bright and ready to learn. I was determined my sheer will was enough to keep me on the straight and narrow.

I was refused private loans having no cosigner and my foster care grant fell through, so I was stuck with the bill of $5,000 for the quarter after the grants were deducted. I had to pay half of that up front. Keith and I had run through a lot of money buying a home studio and Keith had been sending large amounts of my money to his daughter's mother, which I only found out about much later. Leaving my pockets the most shallow they had been in two years.

I was dancing, but it didn't bring in half as much it being the peak of a recession, but still—it would have been enough had I just been supporting myself and not Keith and his extended family. I had $1,500 after my next month's bills were paid and didn't know how I was going to swing the first down payment, when my mom and stepdad offered to loan me the other $1,500.

"I know we haven't always understood each other and things have been hard but—you're my daughter. I want to see you succeed and, Katerbug—I am so proud of you."

Another tear fell from my stormy eyes and splashed onto my jeans, leaving a splatter proof of emotion, as my mother's voice echoed over the receiver of the phone. I had called her crying in defeat. I was trying so hard and it felt like the innumerable odds were stacked against me yet again. I couldn't catch a break. As much as we had been through, I never gave up hope that one day we would heal. I don't care what anyone says. It doesn't matter what had happened before, a little girl lived inside of me who so craved her mother's love. Her approval and acceptance.

I wanted a *mom*.

I couldn't watch a Lifetime movie without being brought to tears because the depiction of the mother-daughter relationship was one that shattered me.

Why can't I have that?

I tried numerous times to give up, to not care. For her opinion to hold no weight in my scales.

But they held the most.

She had the power to build me up as superhuman or destroy me to ash with a single word. I don't know that she ever knew her power. I think she thought I hated her. Maybe that theory was no more than a projection of her feelings for her mother, who abused then abandoned her as a young child, creating the cycle of generational trauma that would repeat with me.

I didn't.

I loved her more than anything, but I built a wall because of said fact. I did, however, blame her.

I should've split the blame between both my parents equally, but I so naturally excused my father because he was so fucked up. He was never a valid option to source love or security from and I knew that my whole life without having to be told. But my mom? She was strong. She had potential and in my child eyes—she failed me.

Over the last year seeing me blossom into the woman I was now, she had begun to reach out. At first I was suspicious and scared, but the child inside of me won over. It always did. We talked on the phone and I sent her my new songs I had been recording in the studio.

You see, I had slammed the door on my heart long before when it came to her. Every new scar with her name on it required a new lock and bolt. But the opposite was also true. With every positive exchange—I'd take a chain off.

It took a while, but soon the barricades were whittled down to none and I let her in again.

"Are you serious?" I asked, dumbfounded.

I would have never asked her. The sheer fear of being told no in a time of desperate need, when I never asked anyone for anything, was enough to break me, so I didn't dare.

"It's a loan—I just want to make that perfectly clear—but we don't care if you just send us twenty dollars a month. As long as you're making an effort to make good on it—that's good enough for us."

I felt a click.

I imagined my heart was a Rubik's Cube that was complete at birth. Each new trauma disorganized the squares more and more, until it became this jumbled mess that my chest held now. It *baffled* me. Every time I tried to reorganize it, I just tangled it more, frustrating me to the point that if I could have, I would have ripped it from my chest and thrown it at a wall. I had tried every therapy known to man to no avail and so I just let it be.

But every once in a while, ever unexpected, I would feel a click. A part of my heart would rearrange into a new form. Still a disaster of mismatched squares—but still. One click closer to being complete. This was one of these moments. Was she the Lifetime mother that I fawned over? No. Not in the slightest. She didn't know what that was because she didn't have that. But she was trying. That was enough for me.

* * *

I was excelling in school. To be honest the Musicians Institute was somewhat of an expensive hack. The talent pool was lacking, due to most of the students being foreign from countries that paid for education fully. But it did offer meetings with A&Rs that I wouldn't have otherwise gotten. The students that had been attending for years discouraged other students from taking the meetings.

"You're wasting your time. They don't actually do anything."

I thought to myself with a slight air of ego—*Maybe you just aren't good enough.*

In the back of my mind, my imposter syndrome would take over and I would be not good enough too, but I shoved it down and barreled on headfirst with such a delusional optimism that I shocked even myself.

I set up a meeting with an A&R for Interscope records. His name was Tunji.

The Musician's Institute, Hollywood Blvd, November 2010

The room was cold and so was the energetic air. The black walls were covered in plaques and certificates and Tunji sat at the desk tapping a pencil, as I sat wringing my hands, trying my best not to look nervous.

The meeting took place in a small building across the street from MI, in the music business degree program's space. Tunji was nice and smiled, but he was bored in every sense of the word.

Obviously, nothing had lit him up before my time slot.

He casually looked at his watch and rubbed his forehead, giving the impression that he was counting the minutes. I handed him a burned CD with my two best records and he slipped it into the production setup before grabbing up the headphones, stiflingly a sigh, and pressing play.

My mind ran rampant as it tended to do. The vibe didn't feel inviting in the slightest. I assumed he was prepared for more disappointment and had resigned to just going through the motions before placating the student and sending them on their merry way, dreams crushed. I imagined it must be a hard gig, having to tell hopeful musician after hopeful musician that they were "Not what we're looking for right now."

I observed with shaky hands and a tapping foot that I quickly stilled once I noticed its frantic thump.

Calm. Just be calm.

I searched his facial expressions, praying they'd give me some sort of clue as to what he was thinking. I didn't have much hope, but the little bit I did have scoured his posture for any sign of emotional reaction.

Wait for it ... Wait for it ... THERE!

His eyebrows furrowed and his head tilted slightly to the left. He was listening now. Not just hearing and there *is* a difference. I could always tell the moment someone switched from hearing to listening. And *he* was listening. There was only one more thing that needed to happen.

THERE! He's nodding his head! HE'S ACTUALLY NODDING HIS HEAD!

I was screaming inside my mind.

Oh my God! He likes it!

His facial expression twisted into something that would resemble the smelling of a foul odor as he bobbed to the beat. Now, normally that would seem to be a bad thing but—not when you're judging music.

That face is the highest compliment only surpassed by the actual words "This is *amazing!*" that would follow.

Tunji removed the headphones from his head and stared at me with the alien stare I had grown so used to hating. Except, I didn't hate it this time. It made me feel special, unique. I sat wide-eyed, holding my breath in an attempt to not hyperventilate and he flashed a grin.

"I don't get to say this too often so I'm gonna enjoy it," he said through a laugh. "This is *amazing*! This is something I can really work with!"

"*Really?*" I couldn't hide the shock in my response.

"Yeah, really. I think I know just where to put you. I know a small publishing label that's looking for a demo singer. They might be the perfect home for you. Now, I can tell you're raw and they can throw some seasoning on ya to get you prepared because this …" He pointed to the CD that had just been popped out of the hard drive. "This is *real*. This is something to be proud of."

"Ah crap! You're gonna make me cry … shit … I mean! Crap!"

Tunji laughed.

"It's cool, it's cool. This is a big moment. Remember it—cuz it's just the beginning."

We exchanged cards and as he slid my disk off of the desk to hand it back to me, he paused.

"Can I keep this?"

"Um—yeah! It's yours. I'll even make you a few more!" I said with a bewildered laugh.

"Hahaha, no—that's not necessary. But, if you could download all of the music you have so far into MP4 and send it to me at the email on my card, I would really appreciate that."

"Of course! I'll get on it! You'll have it tonight!"

When I floated out of that meeting, my heart was flying so high, the toes of my shoes dragged along the pavement as I drifted like a cloud back to my car. I didn't want to come back down to earth.

Was this really happening? Was this Podunk, white trash, felon, junkie, foster-kid, hooker really gonna get a shot?

I had always seen myself as a gutter kid. Someone who had to fight, scratch and claw their way out before the current carried them down a sewer drain, but I was due for a change in the winds. This was it.

I had lucked out on the parking situation and found a meter just feet from the student entrance on McCadden place. I almost hopped in the car, but my anxiety mixed with sheer thrill indicated a celebratory cigarette was in order. I lit up and took a deep ragged inhale, as nicotine rushed through my bloodstream, creating a warm buzz that flushed from my head to my toes.

I heard a cough coming from right beside me.

"Oh shit, I'm sorry!" I said to the towering linebacker of a man, standing on the corner, not three feet away. He didn't look amused.

"You know that shit will kill you?" was his dry response.

"Yeah, that's what they say. But I heard a more important person say, 'Judge not lest ye be judged,' so—there's that."

He cocked his eyebrow, giving Suge Knight vibes.

"I'm Keta," I said, reaching out my fist. "You go here?"

"Chase," he said with a quick dap. "Yeah, I'm a producer."

"Well this must be our cute meet because I'm a songwriter," I said, full of charm.

"A cute what?" He still didn't smile.

So serious, this one.

I didn't mind. Nothing could ruin my night. I was floating on a pink cloud. He was just an extra in a scene of my life I would replay over and over in the coming days.

"A cute meet. You know—it's like the awkward way that two people meet in movies that eventually leads to a lifelong friendship? A cute meet."

"Mm-hmm …"

"Well I gotta go, but"—I pulled one of my freshly printed business cards out of my wallet—"here's my contact if you ever wanna collab."

My words sat in the air like a game of hangman. He took the card, as not to be rude, but left the niceties to lie. I shrugged it off, flicking my cigarette butt into the street, threw up my index and middle fingers, hopped into my car and drove off.

Chapter Sixteen

North Berendo St, Hollywood, CA, November 2010

The drive home was an out-of-body experience. I parked without complaining that the nearest spot I could locate was three blocks away, ran to my complex, punched the code in so frantically I failed the first three times, then flung open the gate and rattled up the stairs to my apartment. I barged in startling Keith, who was watching basketball, as was his life's mission it seemed, with Harlem at his feet.

At my entrance Harlem jumped up and bolted toward me, unable to contain her excitement that I was home. I collapsed onto the floor, as I normally did, to hug her and rub her down as excited to see her as she was me. Her whole butt wagged so hard she could barely keep her back legs on the ground.

"You look happy," Keith said with a smile.

"I am! I met with that A&R and he *loved* my music!"

"No shit?!"

"*Loved* it! Kept my CD and told me to email him all of my songs in MP4 and that he was going to link me with a publishing house out in Tujunga Canyon called Baby C or—Baby G." I paused, trying to remember. "Something like that. Anyways, yeah! *Best meeting ever!*"

"That's dope, you know I'm not surprised, I been—"

"Oh! I gotta send him the songs!" I cut him off, released myself from under Harlem's paws and ran to the Mac, sitting in the corner of my home studio. I did everything frantically. So much so that Keith came up behind me and started rubbing my shoulders.

"Calm down, you good. Just breathe. The email gone get there. Just breathe."

I took a deep inhale and spun the chair around to face him.

"This is big." My eyes wide as I looked up at him.

"It is. We should celebrate."

"Oh yeah? What did you have in mind?"

"Well we still got those Six Flags tickets you won on the radio. How about we do that this weekend?"

I had been driving home from none other than Garden Grove's own 'Larry Flynt's Hustler Club one night, at three in the morning, and had stopped in the Jack in the Box drive-through, when the announcer came over the radio on Power 105.9.

I was in no shape to drive, but was coherent enough to deduce that the odds of being the only one listening to the radio at three in the morning were pretty high. I won the tickets.

"We could do that. I've never been to an amusement park before."

"Really?" Keith said in surprise.

"Yeah … I mean … My dad pretended to take us a couple times, but really it was just his way of getting us in the car so he could kidnap us."

I reached for Keith's open Fanta and proceeded to take a sip with an utter nonchalance, as he stared at me, mouth gaping.

"You're for real right now?"

"I didn't tell you about that?" I said over my shoulder, having refocused on my task of sending the email.

"Yeah no ... you forgot to mention that one." An emotion I couldn't identify filled his tone. "Man, I swear to God, Kay ... sometimes the stories you tell me are like a page in a book."

I hit send and was gone.

* * *

HONCUT, CA, JULY 1998

We ran down the stretch of deserted highway, not knowing our direction, with fear in our eyes as they poured tears down our flushed cheeks. My skinned knees still fresh with scabs, I could feel them breaking open as my feet tore down the gravel, kicking a trail of dust into my sister's face.

"STOP!" she screamed.

Her desperation filled my ears as my feet slowed beneath me and I knew. I knew she wouldn't go on.

It was always her idea. Running away. It wasn't hard to convince me that anywhere was better than here. But, the there we were running to didn't exist. And, those who said "there's no place like home" had never been to mine.

My father had kidnapped us from our mother, not weeks before. My mom was still recovering from yet another tragedy, her fiancé Rick passing away a few months prior. One day he was fine, the next she forced him to go to the hospital and within hours, he was pronounced dead. He had drunk himself to death. She was holding herself together with tape and glue, trying her best to keep things afloat—when my dad showed up with promises of a trip to Great America for the weekend.

Maybe he feigned sobriety well enough to skate past her suspicions. Maybe she just didn't care because she needed a break. Either way, she let us go under the condition that we would be back after the weekend.

We weren't. My father had no intention of returning us. With us in his custody, he could receive government benefits and he was one to play the system.

He lived in a beat-up trailer in Honcut, CA, with his junkie girlfriend Deborah and her three young children—the youngest being two and the oldest being eight. The girlfriend was a certified psychopath.

One time I was playing with my doll in the backseat of the car when she started screaming that I was a witch and was putting a spell on her. My sister and I sat frozen, paralyzed in the backseat, pleading my innocence. I was dragged from the car by the collar of my shirt and told I was going to be left on the side of the road. My father convinced her after an hour that I wasn't a sorceress, but a terrified nine-year-old girl, simply playing with her doll.

Meth does things to your brain and they had a tendency to liquefy it and bang it into their arms as often as they could afford to. Which was more, now that they had us.

This particular day we had built up the courage to escape. I remembered the pain that cracked through my heart, knowing Deborah's kids were trapped there, but Jamie and I promised each other we would send someone for them, once we were safe. We must've been a mile down the road when Jamie stopped in her tracks.

"MEME—LETTT'SS GOOOO." I tugged her arm forward, but released it at her wince. The bruises. We had bruises and welts that covered the better part of our backside as well as our arms, which were less intentional but more defensive wounds.

"I—I have a bad feeling about this—" she told me, tears streaming down her face.

"Look, I know you're scared, but we can't go back there!" I pleaded with her. "Please don't make me go back there!" Jamie grabbed me in her stick-thin arms and hugged me tight, my tears bleeding dark, wet spots into her dirty hand-me-down T-shirt. Cars whooshed past, almost blowing our tiny frames away with the gust. The world was scary. But not as scary as that house.

"I just—I have a bad feeling … like … we're gonna die," she said through sobs.

"We'll die if we go back." I broke at the sight of her, confirming my worst fears. I couldn't let her go back alone. We were all we had and we protected each other.

"No, we won't! Don't say that! I'll protect you!"

I knew there was no way her eleven-year-old hands could defeat the wrath of my father jacked on crank, but also knew the odds were worse without us being a united front.

We took the longest walk of my life back to the trailer where my dad was standing in the front yard, screaming at us as we approached. We held each other tight by the arm and knew as long as we were together, we were OK and nothing, and I mean nothing, could tear us apart.

That didn't mean he didn't try though.

My dad snarled as we approached, holding our tears in. Crying would make us appear weak. We wore the dry salt water on our cheeks, like warrior paint.

Hold on. Just hold on.

Our refusal to let go sparked rage within him as he tried to separate us. We held on tighter.

Don't let go. Never let go.

We fell into the gravel sobbing, our tiny elbows gashed from sharp rocks as we fell as one entity.

Don't let go. Just hold on. We're gonna be OK.

My sister's whimpers quieted as my father screamed something inaudible from over the top of us and pointed inside. Suddenly my hearing worked again.

"GOOOO!" he bellowed.

Jamie and I rose timidly to our feet and instead of taking the straight line into the house within arm's reach of my father, we made our way in a circle, still clutching each other to the point of our fingernails leaving impressions on one another. Once through the door, we ran to the back room, where we huddled in the corner together. My dad approached the door resembling a possession of himself. A void and dead-eyed stare.

This wasn't the dad I loved. This was a demon.

"Deb and I are leaving! YOU STAY IN THIS FUCKING ROOM. I RIGGED THE DOOR SO I'LL KNOW IF YOU LEFT." The trailer shook as he slammed the plywood into the doorframe. A quiet click followed a scratching sound and then he was gone.

"What do you think it is this time?" I asked Jamie, my voice still shaking.

"A sock on the doorknob?"

"No, it was up high … a penny? On the top?"

"Maybe … but if it is, we're gonna have to have Jonathan put it back."

Jonathan was Deborah's oldest son. We sat quietly, making sure the coast was clear, before we attempted to emerge to search the cupboards for food. I clutched my foot. My adrenaline had dispersed and it was now throbbing, as it typically did.

My foot had a large gash in it from stepping on an aluminum can, slicing it open to the tendon, that was horribly infected. I could smell it through my shoe. I untied my laces and pulled off my beat-up Payless brand hand-me-down sneakers to get a better look at it.

Did I rip it back open running?

Blood and pus lined the area of the sock covering the gash. I traced it with my tiny index finger. It was stiff in the center, having soaked through. I had an urge to change my socks, but there weren't any clean ones anyways and I could tell the fabric was glued to my wound. Ripping it off would hurt. I wasn't capable of inflicting more pain on myself at the very moment.

We waited. We were almost sure the coast was clear when a voice came through the door.

"Jamie!" It was Jonathan. Poor kid. My dad was bad, but Deborah? Man, that woman was ten times worse. He cracked open the door and stuck his head in through the slit. His stringy, black, unkempt hair hung in his frantic eyes. Unbathed with skin the color of a bruised pear, his voice shook as he spoke.

"Someone is here!"

"Where?" Jamie said, bolting up.

"At the door! A man and a woman."

"What do they look like?" Jamie asked.

"I don't know. The guy has a beard ... and ... and short brown hair and ... and a hat."

The sound of knocking filled the air, as the unknowns rapped on the thin trailer door. Fear coursed through my veins. The door had been broken into so many times it wouldn't take much effort to kick it in. What if they were here to hurt us? What if my dad ripped someone off and they were here seeking revenge? I could hear my heart beating faster as my mind raced with frames of worst-case scenarios.

Jamie and I looked at each other, speaking in silent sister language, both ending the telepathic sentence with a shake of our head. We didn't know who it could be. Francis, my dad's sponsor, had a beard but he had long hair and didn't wear a hat.

"What's the woman look like?" Jamie inquired.

"She's umm … she's tall … red hair … curly."

Jamie and I took one knowing look at each other before bolting up, screaming "MOM!" as we ran to the front door.

We flung it open and ran to our mom, almost knocking her over. The sunlight fell over her as if it were a halo.

She's here. I knew she would find us. We're safe. She's here.

We cried and my mom hid her horror at the sight of us and ushered us into the backseat of an old Riviera.

We were safe.

* * *

NORTH BERENDO ST, HOLLYWOOD, MAY 2011

I woke up with bile violently making its way up my esophagus and into the back of my throat. I sputtered and coughed as I sat up.

What the fuck was that? I thought as I attempted to gulp back the putrid liquid. I barely had my feet on the floor before the stomach acid I had just swallowed forced its way back up with a vengeance. I shot up and ran to the bathroom with my palm clamped over my mouth to contain the vomit but to no avail. I had just flung open the bathroom door and dropped to my knees when another convulsion in my gut pushed the puke out of my mouth, through my teeth and fingers, and sprayed a yellow, chunky mess all over the back of the toilet seat.

I didn't have time to wipe it off before I hurled again. I threw open the lid and released the demon-like essence that plagued me.

What the fuck did I eat? Was I sick? Couldn't be; I felt fine yesterday. Well, at least most of the day. I hurled again. And again. I'm sure I had a certain je ne sais quoi sprawled in front of the toilet like a drunk teenager with my face pressed against the seat.

Thank God, Keith had just cleaned the bathroom.

"Bae?"

Speak of the devil.

"What's going on?"

His hand tried to push my hair out of my face. "Oh—don't touch—" I wretched again before I could finish the sentence. I had always been sensitive to touch when I was nauseated. This was no exception.

"Shut the door. I'll be out in a minute." I couldn't with him just yet. I wasn't the morning-est person and especially not when I woke up puking my literal guts out.

"You're kinda blocking the door," he replied.

I scooted my knees up and made way for him to grab the handle and gently pull it shut behind him. I sat for a moment, gathering my bearings. It was doubtful there was anything left in my stomach to throw up whether it wanted to or not, but I sat in wait, prepared for another heave. It didn't come.

I picked my head up off the now sticky plastic with a weak neck and wiped my mouth with one of my matching "guest" towels. We didn't have any guests. I just got them because that's what normal people did and though I was far from normal, I pretended well.

I stood up on wobbly legs and felt the whoosh of an uncanny sway. I regained my balance by clutching on to the small vintage-style porcelain sink.

Why am I dizzy?

I looked in the mirror at my frame. I had run to the bathroom wearing nothing but bra and underwear. My breasts. They were gigantic.

"Oh, no!" I let the words escape my mouth, not knowing how loud I was speaking. Keith popped the door open and peeked through.

"You good?"

"No, I'm fucking pregnant."

"What?"

"I'm *fucking* preg-a-nent-ah. Did you understand me that time?"

"How you know?"

I pulled up my bra and my heavy bosom fell out swollen and twice their normal size but still perfectly in place. They looked like bolt-ons.

"I don't get it?" Keith's face curled into confusion.

"Just go get me a test please!" I said with irritation.

"I'll go in a minute."

"KEITH. I HAVE TO PEE NOW AND THE FIRST PEE IS WHEN YOU'RE SUPPOSED TO TAKE A TEST, SO JUST GO NOW PLEASE."

"Fine, but you gonna have to cool it with the attitude when I get back cuz I'm not doing the mood swings today, Kay."

I collapsed on the couch as he grabbed his wallet and made his way out the door.

"Get the one with the lines, not the digital!" I hollered toward the door as it shut behind him.

Fuck.

Now was not the time to wind up with child. Things were moving quickly and I was making quite a name for myself in some very important rooms. I had quit school due to getting an unofficial internship at the publishing house I was demoing for and was working with some pretty high-ranking producers. I had a four-person management team and was pitching songs to major label artists weekly. This was my chance.

I still took high-end clients from time to time and danced on the weekends, but not a soul knew. Except Keith. And Melissa. Melissa was a girl I had met at a mansion party a year or so back. (Yeah … that's a thing.) She was a washed-up junkie porn star but I had no room to judge. She brought me high-paying clients for a small fee and we became fast friends.

I slid my hands down my face and let out a groan before noticing a weed bottle sitting on the end table. Yep. That's what I needed. I might be pregnant but in about fifteen minutes, I might know I was pregnant and for sure wouldn't be able to smoke, so this was potentially my last blunt for nine months. I twisted up the stinky herb and took a large inhale.

Instant calm flooded my system.

Ah … weed. I thought. They should have a commercial for weed— and in it, it's just a girl who takes a hit of a blunt and says, "Ah … weed." The end.

That's how I knew I was high. I was making up commercials for weed in my head. Weed being a scheduled substance that in no way could be marketed, let alone have a commercial.

I giggled to myself, almost forgetting my predicament, when Keith walked back through the door carrying a slack CVS bag.

Fuck again.

Reality hit me in the face with one glance at it.

"Want it?" I said, holding the blunt in the air.

"Good you smoked cuz I was about to knock ya head off your shoulders," Keith said playfully.

"You wouldn't dare, pussyfoot," I joked back.

We laughed. I exchanged the blunt for the bag and disappeared into the bathroom. This wasn't my first pregnancy test. I peed on the stick and waited. The two minutes or 120 little seconds felt like an eternity.

No. Fuck. Is that a line? Which line is the regular line? That's just the regular line. The not pregnant line. OK. We're good.

Wait. What the fuck is that? Is that another line? Please, God, tell me that's not another line.

My internal dialogue was screaming. It was. It was another line. A big fat pregnant line. I was pregnant. I emerged from the bathroom and threw the stick at Keith.

"Hey, man! There's piss all over that!" he said, letting it fall to the floor. "What's it say?"

"Look—"

"I don't know how to read this shit!"

"There are clear instructions written right on the plastic; it's not rocket science."

His face fell as he looked at it.

"So ... what you gonna do?"

"I don't fucking know." I rubbed my forehead with a strength that should have erased the defiant lines worming their way across.

"I just ... I don't think this is the right time to be bringing a kid into the world."

"Yeah, me neither, but it's not you that's gonna have to go through the trauma of getting it ripped from your womb so—I'd chill on the opinions for now."

I didn't want to get an abortion, though I was fervently pro-choice. Mainly because I was anti-government. All the havoc they had wreaked on me my entire life, I'd be damned if I voted for them regulating my body. I had never voted in my life because again, I don't believe in the government. But, that's another story.

I didn't know what to do. I took all of the factors into account. Keith wasn't exactly a star parent to the children he did have, which was the first thing on the con list. He had one kid he barely knew at all and one that I had raised for about six months, so I had a pretty good scope of his parenting style. He had a heart, but he was a drill sergeant deep down and mistakes weren't allowed. Kids make mistakes. A lot of them. I couldn't imagine having my child, the person I would love most, being subjected to that kind of scrutiny.

The other thing that quickly tallied the con list was money. My source of income required that I be hot. I'm pretty sure pregnancy was a faux pas in the industry and aside from a few fetishists, I wouldn't have much luck paying the bills.

Keith didn't work. He had gotten some shit part-time job at Macy's after ten thousand fights about him not working, but it was a sham. It brought in a few hundred bucks a month at most and he only did it so I'd stop hounding him.

What were we gonna do? Live at his mom's in the jungles? No, thank you.

Not only that but—I was inches from my big break. I could feel it. I didn't come this far and go through all of this shit to only come this far. I knew what I had to do. I couldn't find a reason to keep it other than the deep sense of connection I already had with the clump of cells multiplying rapidly into a human within me. But the last thought was the final nail in the coffin.

What if I'm not a good mom?

I could never forgive myself if my child endured even part of what I had and honestly, I just didn't trust myself with such responsibility. So I made the appointment.

* * *

Planned Parenthood, Los Angeles, CA, May 2011

Keith drove me to the clinic and we sat shivering in the cold, depressing waiting room. I felt a darkness enter my soul that mirrored the energy in that place. Like an indoor graveyard with a frigid and haunted draft. As if sadness was built into the foundation.

"Kuns?" I heard my name echo through the still. I thought the doctor was calling my name, but it was coming from my right. Should've known it was someone who knew me. No one pronounced my name right on the first try. I turned to face a familiar-looking stranger.

"Ruiz?" I said, stunned. What were the odds? Two chairs away sat a fellow teenage inmate from forgotten pages of my story's previous chapters.

Ruiz was all but spasming, she was so spun out. Dark pick marks covered her face and arms, the void in her eyes only outshined by the blue and purple bruising around it. We had been locked up together in VYCF for years. The girl I knew resembled Sofia Vergara, timeless beauty, impeccably delicate features. A Latin rose. This version of her was withered, dry and sparse. Her lush petals had fallen off in the cold, harsh frost of life. Now, she was nothing but thorn and stem.

"What the fuck, man, how have you been?" I asked, not able to hide my astonishment.

"Not great, but hey, I'm free you know. Just doing the damn thing," she replied, her jaw doing that weird twitchy thing it does when you've been up far too long.

She needs a nap. A nap and a sandwich.

"What happened to your eye?"

"My baby daddy—that's why I'm here. We lost the first one to DCFS. I'm trying to get her back but she's in a foster home in Reseda and this motherfucker won't stop beating my ass so—I'm just waiting to get into a domestic violence shelter. You know how it is."

I didn't. Thank God, I didn't.

"So … you're pregnant with his kid again?"

"Yeah. He punched me in the stomach when we got in the fight, but nope. Still pregnant, so. That's why I'm here."

Hearing those words uttered with such nonchalance should have been shocking. They weren't. This was hardly the first time I had heard such a tale. No judgment entered my mind. Just sadness. My heart was broken. I'm sure this was a similar fate for a lot of the girls that got out of VYCF. I definitely wasn't in the best situation. I also I wasn't sitting tweaked out with a black eye, waiting for a bed in a DV shelter, was while my kid sat in a foster home in the valley, so. That had to count for something.

Looking at her made me feel like I was making the right choice. I had my dad's genes and was prone to substance abuse.

What if this was me in three years? It could've been me. Statistically, should've been me. But it wasn't.

"Kuns?"

This time it was the doctor.

"Hey! I gotta go."

"No prob, girl. Hey, make sure you tell them to give you extra when they put you out. Sometimes you wake up when they're not done and it's kinda freaky."

I was horrified.

What did she mean *sometimes*? How many abortions had she had?

Her words echoed through the chambers of my mind as I walked back trembling to the procedure room.

"Do you want to see the sonogram?" the nurse asked dryly.

"No." I could feel myself systematically shutting down. Repressing in advance.

"Do you want to know if it's twins?"

"What the fuck, lady?"

Why would I want to know if it's twins, you nitwit, I thought to myself. It was like she heard me because she quickly responded.

"Standard questions, ma'am, you have to answer."

"All no. Please don't make this more real for me."

She blinked, looking irritated and shut the curtain with a jerk, yelling, "The doctor will be in in a minute," from the other side.

Chapter Seventeen

North Berendo St, Hollywood, CA, late June 2011

Everything else was a blur. Keith drove me home and I locked myself in my bedroom for two days. I made him sleep on the couch and only came out to use the bathroom and refill my water bottle. I hated him. I didn't mean to. It wasn't a choice. The abortion it ... it did something to me. All those Rubik's pieces that had clicked back into place were now thrown into a new disorder. I thought I was prepared for the emotional consequences of my actions, but I wasn't.

A part of me died inside. The light behind my eyes went out. I sulked around a shell of myself for days before I knew I had to snap out of it. I put on my best face and went to my sessions and performed like a dancing monkey, only to return to my bed and sleep. I was in the dark, fumbling around for a light switch that didn't seem to exist. It was about two weeks later when my phone rang with a call that would change the course of my future without any warning.

It was Mel.

"Hey, bitch."

"What's up, girl; what's good with you?"

"I got a client for you."

"Oh, yeah? What's the deal?"

"Forties, handsome, Jewish guy, lives in the hills, could be a regular thing. I showed him your pics and he wants to see you tonight."

"Did you talk numbers?"

"I thought I'd leave that up to you, but he knows my fee so he's not unprepared."

"Cool."

"Well, you wanna get together tonight after?"

"I just got that procedure so I'm still reeling, but I miss you. We'll link soon, I promise."

"OK, mamas—feel better, let me know how it goes."

"I will, thank you." I blew a kiss over the receiver and dropped the phone.

I hadn't showered in days and I still couldn't say the word abortion. Procedure was all I could manage. It probably wasn't in my best interest to take clients during the healing process, but I felt like I didn't have a choice. I had to keep the boat afloat. I'd worked too hard to build it and if I didn't keep it all paid for, nobody would. My phone buzzed. It was his contact. Ben.

Doubtful that was his real name but I didn't care. He wouldn't know my real name either. I dialed his number into my text messages, typed a quick message and hit send. He texted back before I could put the phone down. I spent the next few minutes working out the details with him and had a date set up for seven that evening.

Money and the studio were the only reasons I'd get out of bed. Keith didn't understand what I was going through but I growled at him every time he even thought to mention anything, so he quit trying.

What time is it? Five?! Shit! I slept till five!

It would take me an hour in traffic to get there even though it was only five miles away. I rushed to the shower and was ready in a flash.

"Where you going?" Keith asked, pausing his NBA2K.

"Gotta date."

"From Mel?"

"Yep."

My sentences fell short with him. I have a feeling he sensed he was losing me so he had tiptoed around me the past few weeks. Great instincts that one. I took one last look in the mirror, grabbed my keys and was out the door.

* * *

Mullholland Dr, Hollywood Hills, CA

The traffic was thick as molasses and moved at a slow crawl down Fountain Avenue during rush hour. Any motivated snail could have beaten me there. Luckily I wasn't in a race with any snails, but time, well that was another matter. Clients in LA didn't typically mind if you were a few minutes late. Anyone who has ever lived in Los Angeles knows that appointments are approximate at best. You could leave an hour before and hit construction or an accident and be held up for hours.

I, however, loathed being late for anything. Punctuality was a weird symptom of my OCD and it still managed to apply itself even to things I didn't remotely care to do. I'm sure this came from my pure disdain for waiting for people and I wouldn't get to hate people who were chronically tardy if I was one. Strange, the psyche, isn't it? I managed to pull up at the humble mansion's massive and ornate iron gate, right on time.

I parked a few car lengths down, as is customary for any working girl. Horror stories of being tracked, followed and killed plagued me, so I always took extreme precaution. I had clients I had known for years who still didn't know what I drove.

I began my traipse up the street, the click of my heels filling the quiet night air to the end of the cul de sac with my phone pressed to my ear. It was ringing.

"Hello?" A thick accent came over the line.

"I'm here."

"I'll open ze gate."

"K." I hung up and walked slowly as not to be forced to stand dilly-dallying outside for any length of time. It opened just as I approached. I was three steps in the drive when I saw a tall, handsome silver fox waving toward me from the right side of the house. I clicked my heels down the stone walkway and into his arms, greeting him with a warm embrace.

"Wow, you are more ze beautiful zen ze pictures."

His sparkling green eyes gave me a once-over.

"Thank you," I replied with a sultry smile.

"Up ... we go up ze stairs."

"You lead the way."

We made our way through the house to the huge bedroom. The bedroom alone could have fit my entire apartment inside of it. It was decorated in cream, black and gold and looked as if Versace did his interior design. The room wasn't noisy just ... outspoken. I tossed my purse on the bed and the gentlemen walked directly to the nightstand

and did a line with a rolled-up hundred-dollar bill before setting the straw-formed bill on a stack of hundreds … presumably for me.

"What's that?" I asked with curiosity. I hadn't had a line in the better part of a year but on this particular day, numbing out seemed like the right way to go. I had a void to fill. A hungry darkness that spawned from the extermination of my unborn child. I was so deeply emptied and I wanted the emptiness gone. I only knew of one instant fix and as luck would have it, it was sitting crushed on his nightstand.

"Oh … I am zo zorry … you like?"

I laughed.

"What is it?" I didn't really care what it was. I would've sniffed glued in that moment if I'm being completely honest. But I didn't want to seem uncultured so I feigned pickiness with my substances as addicts often will to keep up their charade.

"OxyContin … crush …"

Painkillers. I had a lot of pain I wouldn't mind killing.

"Yes, please."

He used a pill grinder and lined up the potent dust for me before handing me the bill.

"Issa strong … I give you half."

"I'm a big girl."

"OK, you say."

I pulled the bill to my nose and inhaled deeply as I did drug math in my head.

If they're forties—half is twenty. Little less than a Roxy, which should do wonders because I have little to no tolerance.

I felt the sweet familiar drip form in the back of my throat and swallowed with my eyes closed before releasing a breath of relief.

"Is good, no?"

"Very."

"I have one better for you."

He disappeared into the closet and returned with a plastic square in his hand.

"Es fentanyl patch. Good for three days."

This guy is the best, I thought.

He lifted up my dress and placed the patch on my lower abdomen near my pubic line.

"So generous," I said through a laugh.

"Yes ... and this—for you." He pointed to the stack of hundreds.

"I'll grab them—I don't think they're going anywhere." In my early days, I'd get the money and stash it as quickly as I could but I learned over time that the good clients that had the potential to become regulars needed an environment that fostered trust to bloom. You had to pretend like the money didn't matter. That ensured you would always get more. Nobody likes to feel like a dollar sign, even if that is the very arrangement.

He began to kiss my neck. I barely felt a thing. Oxy one, me ... a very happy girl. The date went as most do. He searched every square of my body with his mouth like it was some newfound land he was to conquer and left delicate kisses in the most sensitive places. It always struck me as odd that the most attentive men I had ever met were clients. I had grown accustomed to being worshipped. It made me feel powerful and power is a drug like any other. Even if it was a false sense of power, my psyche had manifested to overshadow the tragedy of it all. It was a bittersweet that would live on my lips for years to come.

My limbs were limp and I was high as a kite, one foot in reality, the other in a dream state that I quite preferred. The rise and fall of our bodies felt like I was floating in the ocean. Drifting further and further out to sea.

Would water fill my lungs and be the end of me? Oh, I'd hoped so.

I took a deep inhale and to my disappointment, the water was oxygen.

Just air. Stupid, weightless, necessary air.

I don't know how long I was there and I lay in his bed long after we were done. I was lit like the tip of a cigarette. Suddenly the urge to smoke filled my mind. I rolled over and looked at him. He was ever so still with the exception of his chest, which expanded and deflated, deep and rhythmic.

"I'd hang out for a bit longer, but I promised Mel I'd stop by and help her with some stuff." The lie fell through my lips smooth as butter and sounded much better than the truth of "I need a fucking cigarette and I assume you don't smoke in here."

"I can call you again?"

"Anytime, babe."

"Here, wait here."

He peeled himself up off the plush California king and confidently walked naked into the closet.

His little butt cheeks reminded me of those of cherubs painted on to plates that hung on the walls of my mother's house. I quickly dressed and was fastening the clasp on my pump when he reemerged with a small bottle and set it down on the nightstand next to the cash. I stood and gathered both, stopping for a moment to review the small orange unlabeled pill bottle's contents. There were roughly ten oxys. Smart man. He knew I'd have to come back to get more.

"Didn't they stop making these?" I asked with a curious delight.

"Yes, but I have plenty … I get and stock up when my doctor friend tell me they make no more."

"Well it was wonderful to meet you—I—I'm sorry I never caught your name."

I knew his fake name but I was testing for trust level.

"Ahmed."

"Nice to meet you, Ahmed."

"I walk you down."

He guided me down the stairs and to the place where we met on my arrival. Gave me a hug and a kiss on the cheek goodbye and then opened the gate for me to walk back to my car. I lit a Newport 100 as I exited the drive. Once to my car, I sat on the hood, taking the smoke deep into my lungs while staring up into a starless sky.

I probably shouldn't drive, I thought to myself. But I would. Not remembering much of the drive home, I made it into my house safely, walked directly to the room not speaking a word to Keith, and fell asleep.

* * *

HOLLYWOOD, CA, AUGUST 2011

The next few weeks were spent in a waking coma. On the outside it looked no different to Keith; my depressive episodes so similarly resembled me on copious amounts of opioid narcotics. I often wonder if the pills were what kept me from feeling just enough less pain enough that I didn't end my life because I was teetering on a very close edge.

I was still progressing in my career, taking label meeting after label meeting and was able to paint on my smile and say all the right things but as soon as the curtain closed, I'd take off my pretty mask and dive headfirst into the black.

I didn't want to die but—I definitely didn't want to be alive. Being alive was hard and though I don't believe I would have killed myself, if a bus hit me I'd have been OK with it. OxyContin was the compromise. Like death but without the commitment. Death with benefits, if you will. I floated around my life in a dream state and though I assumed some people knew something was off, there were no blatant indicators that I was about to jump the tracks.

Even I didn't know.

Most of my experiences with substances had made it fairly obvious to myself and others that I was in too deep. This was the first time I had experienced the all too common plague of denial and in my experience, it's the moment that your addiction convinces you you've got it all under control that it's got you under its, and good.

It would make sense due to the fact that doctor-prescribed opiates tend to be the longest tolerated substance in functional addiction. Amhed became a regular and once a week, I'd go back and get my supply.

This went on for months before he told me I had the last of the few OCs known to man in the tiny little bottle in my hand, to which statement my heart fell into my stomach.

Fuck.

I tried to ration the pills out as long as I could but I had a habit of smoking myself into an oblivion. Snorting them was nice and all, but using a bit of spit and toilet paper to rub off the candy coating before plopping them down on a freshly pressed perfect square of tin foil was ten times the rush. But I was running out. I assumed my devil's candy carousel was slowing to a stop and I would just have to hop off the horse and be done with it. Oh, was I wrong.

I sat curled up on my black leather chaise, zoning out on a rerun episode of Friends as I tended to do on my nights off. I was taking more and more nights from dancing in the club, having a few regular clients on my roster and getting utterly sick of my money going missing due to Keith supporting the mother of his daughter with my hard-earned cash. I was lying about how much I was making and he often tried to throw tantrums regarding my working less, to which I waved off without a second thought after saying, "If you don't like it, you can leave."

He was losing me and he knew it.

He even proposed. Bought me a ring with my money. I didn't want him to be in my general vicinity, let alone him touch me. It was only a matter of time now. The pills kept me sedated enough that I was complacent. Just waiting for my big break now. Waiting for all the pieces of my puzzle structured by years of harrowing effort to fall into place and all of my dreams come true so I could finally enjoy the fruits of my labor and until then ... I was gonna be high.

Delusional, I know but—drugs do that to a person.

The commercial filled up the large flat-screen when my phone rang. It was ten o'clock.

Who the fuck is calling me at ten?

It was Mel.

"Hey, girl."

"He—left—me—on the—side of—the highway!" Mel sobbed into the receiver.

"What? Girl, slow down! Take a breath, where are you?" I stood up, my adrenaline pumping. This wasn't the first time Mel had called me to be rescued. I had picked her up from jail on more than one occasion and helped her move out of the place she shared with her pimp, only for her to return to him weeks if not days later. But she was my friend and sometimes you do crazy shit for your friends. Not to mention I was addicted to the chaos of it all. I had grown up in a constant fuck storm of disfunction and this square life, college, successful entrepreneur image I struggled to maintain was boring.

I was subconsciously itching for a mode de sabotage.

"We got into—a huge fight and he—he left me on the side of—the—101 freeway. I just—" Inaudible sobs filled the receiver.

"What exit?"

"Winnetka."

"North or south?" My hyper-focus was in drive. High or not, I always had a knack for keeping my cool in a crisis.

"Umm ... north ... we were going home."

"Try to walk up to the gas station there on the corner. Call me if anything changes but I'm on my way."

I snatched up my keys and purse and was halfway out the door when Keith yelled at me.

"Where you going?!"

I paused for a fraction of a second to look over my shoulder with a glare that I reserved especially for him.

"Don't worry about it," I growled and slammed the door behind me.

* * *

I was there faster than I should have been. Luckily the north side of the freeway was wide open while the south side was in gridlock for miles. Everyone was on their way to Hollywood.

Was it Friday?

I didn't know anymore. I pulled into the gas station and saw Mel's curly blond hair instantly. I skirted forward in her direction and hit the corner like a getaway driver, startling her at first. A look of relief crossed her face as she popped the door and all but spilled into the front seat.

Mel was small with a petite beauty. She grew smaller by the day it seemed if that was even possible. A breath of air could've blown her down. Her big blue eyes were lined in coal and the mascara streaks that lined her cheeks resembled the fat furry legs of tarantulas. Not her best look. I searched in the center console for some wet wipes and tossed them into her lap.

"Thanks, girl," she said, still fighting back tears that flooded eyes with pinpricks as pupils. She blew her nose in a wet wipe and flipped down the visor mirror, gasping at her reflection.

"Oh my fucking God! I'm so haggard, what the fuck."

"You're fine; you've just been crying. Cut yourself some slack, girl."

She sunk in her seat with her head back, trying to calm her ragged breaths.

"Where are we going? My house?"

"No, I have to go home," she said, in more of a moan than a sentence. I gave her another once-over. No bruises I could see with my naked eye but I never trusted that it wouldn't go there with these two. They weren't just toxic. They were *cancer*. Anthrax lovers. The poster children of dysfunctional relationships. I took a deep breath, forming my next question carefully in my mind.

"Is he there?"

"Probably," came her quick and defeated reply.

"Alright, well I'll come in for a minute to make sure everything is cool and he's chilled out. Are you chilled out? Cuz … if not, we can wait till we are. I'm not trying to volunteer myself into a war zone, if I can help it."

"Yeah … I'm chill." She took another breath and started rummaging through the console. "You got a cigarette?"

"Here." I pulled two Newport's out of my pack and lit both, handing her one. "Smoke these; then we'll go."

Mel took a drag, let her head fall back on the rest, locking eyes with me and exhaled.

"Why you so good to me?"

"You got me, man," I said with a laugh, trying to shake the seriousness out of the air. She laughed through her cigarette smoke, choking on it, which resulted in more laughter.

"Hey," I said, brushing a stray lock from her face and behind her ear. "You're good. You're safe."

She exhaled deeply and nodded knowingly. We sat silent in the gas station for a few more minutes, smoke billowing from the car and when we finished our cigarettes, we flicked them out of the window and peeled out.

Minutes later, we were pulling into her driveway. Well, not her driveway; it was a mansion they were crashing at for the time being. Mel had given up her place the last time she left Jaden and now was luxury couch surfing.

Resourceful as fuck that one.

As we walked into the gargantuan house, our footsteps echoed across the marble flooring and through the vaulted ceilings. It was mere seconds later that I knew I had had a terrible lapse in judgment.

"Oh, look who the fuck decide to show up, *this* junkie bitch." Jaden's voice echoed through the house and a look I had only seen once before contorted his handsome face into that of a rabid animal. His words oozed hate as they dripped from his full mouth.

"Hey, hey now ... cool it, let's just keep it cool." I tried my best to moderate but that was a fool's game and I was a glutton for punishment.

"Shut the fuck up!"

Suddenly I realized that hell was tied together by a very thin thread.

And it was about to break loose.

I never wanted to be wrong more in my life. But I wasn't. Had a sixth sense for these things. Mel was the mine that set off the field, to my surprise. She came at him with a wrath I had only seen her display toward him.

Relatable.

"WHO THE FUCK YOU TALKING TO LIKE THAT; YOU'RE NOT GONNA TALK TO MY FRIEND LIKE THAT IN MY FUCK-ING HOUSE, YOU BROKE-ASS FUCKING LOSER!" Mel's five-foot-nothing frame was pressed into Jaden's tower of a waist, challenging him like a rabid Chihuahua. One strong kick and she would've flown across the room but in her rage, she was ten feet tall.

He pushed her. She swung.

It all happened so fast I didn't even notice the dog barking behind me. He went to swing back and I cut in between them like lightning. I was only attempting to break them up but there was no way to communicate that to the eight-month-old pit bull that had sunk its teeth into my calf in the same split instance. In a seamless transition, I dropkicked the pup across the room in sheer reflex, pushed Jaden back toward the couch and threw Mel's seemingly weightless body through the nearby bathroom door. I was one step behind her when a porcelain figurine smashed into the frame, a near-miss of my head.

I froze stunned and enraged for the slightest moment before assessing the large mass that had flung itself off the couch and was now rushing me. I stepped past the threshold and swung the door closed in just enough time to slam it shut behind me. Only a thick oak door separated us from him and his screams penetrated through without any trouble. He kicked the door and we watched wide-eyed as it jumped for well over a minute, both expecting that in seconds he would come barreling through.

But he didn't. That was one strong fucking door.

Once Mel realized the door was holding, she started digging through her bag for a fix. I, on the other hand, was sitting on the sink with the water running, watching chunks of my flesh fall from my calf and swirl down the drain.

"I'm so sorry, girl," Mel said, not once lifting her eyes from the concoction she was mixing with the plunger of a hypodermic needle in a spoon.

"It's cool, she was protecting you; she thought I was attacking her parents. It's just a flesh wound."

Mel had sucked up the tan liquid heroin in her syringe and was now fishing for a vein.

But Mel didn't have any. And Jaden knew it. The kicks stopped only long enough for him to scream, "BET YOU CAN'T FIND A VEIN, CAN YOU, YOU FUCKING JUNKIE BITCH? OPEN. THE FUCK-ING. DOOOOOOR."

"Yeah, that's how to get someone to open a door, genius. Just act like a complete psycho on the other side! Real inviting, you fucking idiot," I replied through my teeth.

"I HOPE YOU STICK YOURSELF A HUNDRED TIMES AND NEVER FIND A VEIN." He was taunting her, trying to send her over the edge and it was working.

"SHUTTT. THE FUCKKK. UPPPPPPPP." Her shrill scream bounced off the bathroom walls as she shook and her face was the shade of red that came stock on eighties corvettes.

"Don't let him get to you. Don't fucking listen. Don't respond. If you respond, it feeds into it. If you don't, he'll get tired."

Hopefully, anyways.

She found a vein. Her face flushed and she started scratching all over her body. It didn't look to me like it felt too good until she let out a sigh of relief and I was jealous of her. I had left my pills at my house and was sitting bleeding out of four puncture wounds. An OC would have taken the edge off.

"You don't have a pill, do you?"

"No, but I have some black." I hesitated.

"I don't shoot."

"Do you have bobby pins?" She was looking at me but one of her eyes just couldn't get it together and drifted away, making her look completely insane with her slack mouth struggling to form the words. They came out in a slur that I had learned to understand only after knowing her for months.

"In my hair? Yeah … what's that—"

She cut me off. "Gimme 'em."

I pulled the two bobby pins out of the back of my hair and handed them to her. She straightened them into sticks.

"See you put it on this one"—she talked her way through her actions every step—"and you light this one … till it's like this … and you do this … voila! Also works with paper clips," she ended her matter of fact sentence, handing me the bobby pins now turned drug paraphernalia.

One thing you can't say about addicts is that they aren't inventive.

I stared at the bobby pins I held in my hand in a moment of clarity.

Do I really want to do heroin?

My heart said no—but the fire-breathing dragon in my mind said yes, and much louder. It spat flames as it roared to be fed. I lit the lighter, satisfying the dragon as I chased it. If only I'd have known that same dragon would soon breathe on everything I so loved—and burn it all to ashes.

Chapter Eighteen

HOLLYWOOD AND HIGHLAND, NOVEMBER 2011

I sat across from Mel in a smoke-filled Maserati parked in the red somewhere off Cahuenga Boulevard. Only the dead were awake at this ungodly hour, the dead and the soon-to-be. We were waiting for a score. Funny thing about dope dealers is they're never on schedule.

We'd been cramped in that car for so long that we'd kicked off our shoes and contorted our bones into awkward-looking yoga poses in the front seat. I had one knee up with my foot on the tan leather and the other thrown across the center console, my foot falling just below the steering wheel. Mel was a fraction of me. She fit like a ball in the center of the driver side's plush seat.

I took another hit of the blunt that was warding off my soon to come withdrawal symptoms as well as my impatience.

"You ever think of what it be like to die?" Mel spoke slowly as if in a daze as she focused in on the blond curl she was twisting around her index.

"You mean clinical depression? Um … yeah, bitch … got that." A grin crawled across my face as I tilted my tired head back on the window, soaking in the melty feeling produced by the weed.

"Nah … I mean like … are you scared? Like … did you do what you came to do? As in like …" Mel ripped the blunt again and finished the sentence, the weed still filling her lungs "If you knew you were about to die … like … what would go through your mind?"

I sat and thought for a moment before taking the blunt from Mel's cigarette-thin fingers. It was gone but I wanted one last hit. I inhaled, pulling the cherry down to my fingertips, burning them slightly.

"Ah fuck!" I yelled, dropping it into my lap with a click of my tongue.

"Bitch! If you burn my seat, I swear to *Gawd!*" Mel said, laughing through the haze.

"I got it, man." I had quickly swept the roach off my skirt and dropped it in an old Diet Coke can sitting in the cupholder.

Where the fuck was this dude at?

"You didn't answer my question." Mel cracked the window as she lit up a Newport.

I reached for her pack and followed suit. I blew out the smoke and replied.

"I mean … that's more than one question so let's break it down into parts."

Mel laughed. "Shut your old SAT high-scoring ass up. Fucking Mensa wannabe-ass bitch."

"Fuck you, Mel, I'm being for real." I laughed through a drag of my cigarette and nearly choked. Hacking and coughing fell in the dips between chuckles and inhales.

"Fuck, bitch, don't die before you answer the million-dollar question … Inquiring minds …" She ashed her cigarette out the window and leaned back against it. "Want to know." Her words curled and swooped through the air as if she spoke in cursive.

"Would I be scared? Nah ... The world I've come to know has been—I mean—exhausting. Death seems like ... a nap, maybe." Mel's head cocked to the side.

"Bitch, you said a *nap?!*" She couldn't contain her laughter. Each giggle that she pushed from her chest had a *k* sound. As if the laugh was reserved especially for me.

"For real, man, I'm tired. A nap sounds good right about now."

"Mm-hmm." The car was now filled with the strong smell of cigarettes. She puffed and puffed, letting the stench of nicotine settle into the $100,000 seats. "And the other part?"

"What would I think if I knew I was about to die?" I replied, my eyebrows contorting into an expression of deep concentration.

"Yeah, man ..." Mel ashed her ciggy again and raised it to her lips as if it were the last she'd ever smoke.

"I mean—I'd be cool. I did everything I could do. I tried. *Always.* I never gave up. I believed even when to believe was delusional. I just—I was *brave.* The whole time I was brave. I coulda quit and I didn't. I never stopped reaching for more and ... I think that's all life is. I'd be sad that I didn't get to see what else I could do but ... yeah. You can't say I didn't risk it all for a chance—I can live with that ..." I paused to take a hit of my Newport that was long overdue. "If I can live with it, then dying with it would be no different right?"

Mel stared at me, ingesting every word as if it were a foreign delicacy. She smiled with her eyes and the corner of her lip jumped ever so quickly before returning to its rightful place. Mel nodded and puffed her stog again.

"You smart as fuck, you know that?" I could barely see her through the smoke now so she couldn't see the nod I offered in agreement. "You hear me?"

I laughed loudly, throwing my head back. It was a real laugh. I didn't get those too often lately.

"Yeah, I heard you, bitch. You said I'm smart. I already know."

"Oh, OK ... you a cocky bitch." The banter continued as the minutes until forever ticked on.

"No, bitch," I said through a scoff, my grin from ear to ear, "I actually know how smart I am."

"Oh yeah, how you know? Just comparing to other people?" Mel had finished her cigarette and was leaning her head back on the window, her eyes barely open. I thought back to another life, it seemed.

"Nah ... when I was a kid; you know how I was in the system?"

"Yeah."

"Well they thought I was crazy so they did all these tests on me to have me committed. Like inkblot tests. IQ tests, all that. Everything came back normal. My IQ was ... high ... shocked the shit out of them."

"How high?" Mel inquired.

"'Bout as high as we are right now, bitch," I said through a laugh.

"That's pretty fucking high," Melanie quipped. We gave each other a knowing look and the car erupted with hardy laughter, spilling through the cracked windows and into the Hollywood night. It took a moment before we regained our composure and as we did, I wiped my favorite type of tears from my eyes.

"Yeah ... anyways ... yeah—that's why I said I knew."

Melanie settled deeper into her seat before inquiring further.

"Did you get committed?" A quick chuckle escaped me and I sighed with a loud *ah* before my reply.

"Wouldn't you like to know?" I toyed with her. She was hanging on every word. I wanted the conversation to end. I never let anyone in this deep. Keith didn't even know this story.

It was my belief that people only want to know your secrets so they could use them as ammunition.

"Bitch, if you don't tell me what happened, I swear to *Gawd* ... shit like a soap opera. Got me all invested in the characters now." The laughter continued to fill the air. I readjusted in my seat, putting my foot up on the dash and straightening my back out. Luckily I was emotionless. Numbed out. Just enough to tell the tale without ripping a mom-sized hole through my chest.

"Nah ... not to the crazy house ... later ... later they put me in CYA for a few years ... but yeah ... I wasn't crazy ... I was traumatized. Most people they send to institutions are just traumatized."

"What you go to YA for?"

"Some dumb-ass shit, man."

"Like?" Melanie was becoming slightly more animated. Not much more. The expected energy level in this car had a pretty low bar.

"Well I got into a few fights and stole some petty shit, but the main charge they got me for was felony forgery when I was eleven."

"The fuck you forge at eleven?" Mel's bewilderment at the charge was one I knew all too well. I felt my soul cringe at the reminiscence, my first visceral reaction since the conversation began. I was starting to feel trapped.

Breathe—just breathe.

"I was selling chocolate ... for my school." I motioned for Mel to hand me another cig. She popped it out of the pack and lit it in her petite pout before handing it to me and lighting up her own. "I only sold seventeen, but in order to go to the pizza party, you had to sell a whole box so ..."

"Shut the *fuck* up." Mel couldn't hide her shock.

"I changed one of the checks to look like I sold a whole box so I could go to the pizza party and ..."

"And the school charged a fucking eleven-year-old with a felony?!" Her outrage was painted thick on her pretty face and still had extra to spare.

"Not the school."

"WHO!"

I waved her off. I didn't feel like talking anymore. But she persisted and showed no signs of surrender.

"Bitch, *who*?! YOUR FUCKING *PARENTS*?"

I didn't reply verbally but cocked an eyebrow and flashed her a knowing look.

"And they locked you up for years for that? ARE YOU FUCKING KIDDING ME?"

"Well not just that ... I was a handful ... I got into fights ... stole some lady's purse ... went through the foster care system and what a fucking joke that was"—I blew a thick cloud from my lungs and the wave of nicotine calmed some of the repressed emotions that had begun to surface—"and then on to group homes ... I'd run away ... get kicked out ... nobody wanted to deal with me so I'd just fuck up from the get and get the process over quicker. It was gonna happen anyways. I was damaged goods. But yeah ... the confinement time they had on me was from the felony forgery. I hadn't committed a crime in a year and a half when I was committed. But I was a ward of the state so ..."

"THEY CAN DO THAT? JUST LOCK YOU UP FOR YEARS BASED ON SOME BULLSHIT?"

"Um yeah, Mel." I couldn't contain my laughter. It was always comical to me that most people have no clue what "government" means. "It's the fucking government ... they can do whatever they want." My cigarette was finished but I wasn't done needing nicotine.

Chain smoke it is.

I grabbed another from the dwindling pack, fit it between my lips to hang from my mouth like a star of an old noir film, and lighting it with the cherry of the cigarette I was to dispose.

"Ya don't *fucking* say." I took in the aghast expression that covered Mel's face.

"Yeah, but boo-hoo. Those were the cards. I'm just playing 'em." Mel fell silent for a second, soaking it in or maybe she was just tired. Either way, we sat without the exchange of words for the better part of a minute.

"But ... you're so—I don't know—*normal*." I choked on my cigarette smoke, erupting in a fit of coughs and laughter. One glance at Mel's face told the tale that she didn't get the joke.

"Um, yeah ... super normal. Sitting in a Maserati with a porn star for two hours waiting for some Russian guy named Z to drop off heroin, when I have a meeting with the VP of Sony Publishing in a week and a pimp sitting at home ... super fucking normal ..." The sarcasm fell from my lips with a bite.

"You know what I mean." She turned and looked straight ahead. "Where the *fuck* is Z!" she exclaimed, finally expressing the feelings I had been fostering since the second we parked.

"No ... I don't ..." I squished the half-smoked cigarette down on itself on the Coke can, making it fold into a dirty two-toned worm and wiping the excess ash smudged on my fingers on my skirt. "And I don't fucking know."

Mel took a drag of her cig and thought in silence for another moment before speaking again.

"You're right," she said softly.

"'Bout what?" I replied.

She looked at me dead in the eye.

"You are brave."

* * *

North Berendo St, Hollywood, CA, December 2011

I fluttered my eyelids open like a butterfly landing on a lily. My groggy gaze danced around my half-cracked lids before landing on a dirty vase of sunflowers long past their expiration date, on the sun-soaked ledge directly ahead. Another leaf fell and floated weightlessly onto the window sill that was littered with dry dust and mustard-colored petals.

I always thought that it was as if when a flower died, it held a wake for itself. I loved that thought. The ones floating around between my ears and behind my eyes at present weren't so beautiful. I tried to blink them back and as I took an inhale, I felt something move by my feet.

Suddenly I was catapulted back into my body from the in-between space I had been swimming in only moments before. My eyes darted to the right and I felt sick as it all registered.

It was Keith. Panic ran through my brittle bones. *Fuck! Fuckety, fuck, fuck! How long have I been here? Where are my ... fuck ... he knows.*

My mind swarmed and attacked like a pissed-off hive of honey bees. Every one of the thousand thoughts that flooded my psyche landed with a sharp sting. As I sat up, looking around frantically for my stash, a char-coal blackened foil slid off of my lap and hit the floor with a metallic *tink*.

I snatched it up ever so suspiciously. I don't know what I was trying to hide; he had seen it I'm sure, so the secret was out. Still a part of me held a childlike hope that I hadn't just been exposed for the junkie I was yet again. Throughout my frantic process of assessment, he remained completely silent, staring straight ahead. His lack of facial expression threw me deeper through the loop I was winding down, mentally unraveling. I could feel my entire world circling the drain as my demons swallowed me whole.

I sat in a stunned silence playing into our famous little game of who would first speak. I felt like prey.

Maybe if I stay real quiet, real still, he'll get bored and go away.

Except that it didn't work for real predators like lions and tigers and bears so it was unlikely that it would work in this instance either. I was playing mental chess with myself while I still had time to figure out what the fuck I was going to say.

What the fuck could I say?

Well with flagrant evidence countering every possible angle I could fabricate, it seemed nothing.

It was checkmate and I knew it. I lose.

Keith turned his face to look at me, staring at him like a deer caught in the headlights. He shook his head gently. I didn't much care what he thought as much as I cared who he'd tell.

How am I going to clean this up? I asked myself.

My refusal to speak only seemed to irritate him more. The air was so thick with tension I felt each inhale get heavier as if I were breathing underwater. Someone had to speak. But what the fuck was I going to say?! At least if he spoke first, I had a leg up. I could twist something he said or refocus upon some unrelated topic and drive it so far away from anything that happened in here tonight, he might forget how the fight started but he had to speak in order for any of those things to be plausible exit strategies. I was starting to squirm. It would have to be me.

"Um … hey." I spoke softly as to check the temperature of the room. Stuck my verbal toe in the water. He cocked his head to the side and blinked in such a way that had I not known him, I'd have thought he was attempting Morse code or on the brink of having a seizure. The experiment served its purpose and proved the waters hostile and unsafe. Good to know.

I was trying to figure out how to follow my first genius sentence when he spat the words,

"Hey? HEY? That's what the fuck you wanna say to me right now?!" from his lips like venom.

I fumbled with different alphabetical sequences, none of them words, before finally coming up with "Um … how … how are you?" I wasn't giving him much to work with, but it wasn't intentional. This was one of the few times in my life I was utterly at a loss for words. I shook my head with a shrug. That did it.

He lost it.

"WHAT THE FUCK ARE YOU DOING, KAY! YOU'RE DAYS AWAY FROM THE BIGGEST MEETING OF YOUR LIFE AND I COME HOME TO YOU LIKE THIS?! LIKE THIS, KAY?! AND WHAT THE FUCK IS THIS? HEROIN!?" He ripped the blanket off of my lap, exposing the tin foil I had foolishly hidden underneath it only minutes before, sending it and the blanket flying through the air.

"HOW LONG HAS THIS SHIT BEEN GOING ON, KAY?"

"I DON'T KNOW!" I screamed in reply. I felt my body fill with shame, which quickly turned to anger as all of my emotions did, boiling up from my gut to spew out of my mouth like a teakettle bubbling over.

"I'M SITTING HERE VOUCHING FOR YOU, TELLING MY BEST FRIEND IN THE WORLD THAT YOU SOLID—"

"I AM FUCKING SOLID!"

"MEANWHILE YOU SMOKING BLACK TAR HEROIN IN OUR FUCKING LIVING ROOM DURING BROAD FUCKING DAYLIGHT—"

I felt myself slipping, losing touch with reality as I screamed the same words again.

"I *AM* FUCKING SOLID!"

"NO, YOU'RE NOT!" His voice shook the room as he slammed his fist into the bookshelf, knocking everything atop it to the floor. The room fell dead silent. We both stared, our chests heaving in sync as he gathered his wits to speak again.

"You're a fucking house of cards." The words shattered me in places I hadn't known could be reached with all of the steely gates I had put up but I threw another chain link among the stacks of iron rods around my pride and fumed silently in response. Maybe the sheer lack of visible fucks given would shock the situation into a reset. I didn't count on it but the unrealistic escape routes in my mind didn't cease from surmounting. I was grasping at dry straws and they were crumbling in my tar-stained fingers.

"You're so close. You worked so hard. I just—I don't fucking get it."

I lit up a cigarette in a house that I didn't smoke in before I replied.

"No, I'm not—"

"YES, YOU FUCKING AR—" I swallowed up his pleads with my shrill tone.

"NO!" My voice carried over his and swelled as it bounced off the walls that seemed to be getting closer by the minute before slipping through the cracks of the window having nowhere else to go.

267

"People like me ... we don't get real chances. We get real close. Disrespectfully close. Just close enough that you can see it all happening, taunting you, but always ... always ... just a touch out of reach. But the truth be told ... I used to not mind. It kept me looking forward. But sometimes ... sometimes, Keith ... fuck that carrot. It will still be there to lead me on when I wake up but for now, I'm tired. I gave all I had and it was a good try! It really was! But it's never going to be good enough." I sucked the nicotine-filled poison into my shallow lungs and held it for the slightest moment before releasing it in a sigh of relief.

Keith looked at me like I was possessed. Maybe I was.

"Are you fucking kidding me right now?" His face fell white like he had seen a ghost. Maybe in that moment, he realized the cold hard truth that he had pushed me too far. Right. Over. The edge. I was so tortured I was willing to just throw it all away if it meant a moment of peace without someone leaching me of not only every dollar I made ... but my sanity. I mean, only a crazy person would do that right? Give up their dream to escape their nightmare?

"I don't expect you ... someone who's obviously never worked for anything so hard in their life ... to get it." He stared at me as he saw the pieces of his fate all fall into place. I was blowing it all up. He'd thought I hadn't the nerve. Too much to lose. News flash, motherfucker, I've started over with nothing so many times, if there's one thing I know how to do, it's that. Just wish I would've believed sooner.

I put out my cigarette in a water bottle and turned to rifle through the stack of mail sitting on the back of the couch. My actions were completely unexpected. Even by me. Something had snapped and I had gone rogue.

I slid a single leaf of paper out of the stack and folded it into a paper airplane. I smoothed the creases ever so perfectly, lit another cigarette in the upturned corner of my mouth and threw the plane in the air. It hit him in the chest as intended, falling to the floor and sliding across it as I filled the room with the sound effects of a crash.

It was the eviction notice. I hadn't paid the rent in two months.

I wasn't even on the lease of the apartment I paid for years so the anticipation of the look on his face when he realized he owed four grand in rent and only his name on the notice warmed me to my soul. I had the means to pay it; I was just done. I had tried to leave him time and again in a decent and respectable manner and was always swindled back in through some loophole.

I had wised up after my last exit strategy failed and gotten another car. This one without him in the paperwork but the apartment was still in his name and now … to make it worse … he was tied into the music, assigning himself as manager in my contract as a prerequisite to me landing the management contract with Frank.

He was embedded in me.

So in order to leave, I'd have to leave everything … and in a single moment, I was finally ready to watch it all crash and burn. He unfolded the paper plane as I stared at him with eyes dark like the Dead Sea and watched salt water fall from his.

"You should start figuring out where you're gonna go." The words crashed into him like the Titanic into the iceberg. His unsinkable ship was on its way down. I watched from outside my body as if on cue the theatrics began to unfold, reminding me just how much he reminded me of my father.

"I'll kill myself if you leave … I can't do this without you!" The threats had gotten old. The Romeo and Juliet allure it once held had faded and now he just sounded pathetic.

How did this man ever have so much power over me?

269

I was sickened by myself but shook it off as quickly as it came. I didn't have time for that now.

"I don't know what to tell you; you wanna go play in traffic, that's your business." The cruel words danced in the air like the hate in my eyes. I always expected this day would come but truth be told, I didn't expect it to come as it did. I guess it's true what they say. When you're done … you'll know.

I did. I was.

I could see panic swiftly fall over Keith's face. This time it was him racking his mind for an angle to spin. There wasn't one.

Well, there were plenty. But none that would work.

"And what, you're just gonna try and take everything? We built this together?!"

My internal voice seethed and hissed. No, you jackwagon. We built this off my back, paying the price with my soul.

But I wouldn't give him the validation of raising my voice again. I wouldn't even fight him on it. He could have it. I hope it stung knowing that I would rather give up damn near everything that I owned and loved than be with him. I hope it killed him. He realized he was losing control and went for the jugular. I was ready for it.

"Fine. I'll tell everyone the truth. I'll tell them you're a junkie. You won't have a career when I'm done with you." He snarled hate, filling his bones, bringing them to life. He was spinning out of control.

"*Do—your—worst!*" Emotionless, my reply. And he would. Oh would he. But I would be rid of him. It all came together for me in the moment of that reply.

Did I subconsciously sabotage because somewhere deep down knew it was the only way? Did I pick up a new habit not only to deal with my current reality but because my spirit knew that for this moment to occur, I would need to be so fucking numbed out that no loss was too great for the chance to start again?

It all came together like an intricate plan. Like I did everything leading up to this point intentionally and yet without my knowing. I let the feeling of freedom wash over me but held it inside. I would still need a way out and these drugs were not it. But I could do it. For the first time, I knew I could do it.

Because I *had to* if I was to salvage anything from the flames.

But for now—I was quite content with watching it burn.

Chapter Nineteen

Four years clean from heroin

Huntington Beach, CA, November, 2019.

"And how does that make you feel?" My therapist's words broke through my thoughts and I looked around the minimalist-styled office as I shuffled my insides around, searching for the right answer to this often repetitive question.

I had picked her based solely on the facts that my insurance covered most of her services and that she had plants in her office. I liked plants. If you can keep plants alive, you're doing better than most of the population. Shows a dedication to things outside yourself without the need for reward to care. I knew because I had nearly twenty of my own.

Her name was Janet, which hardly seemed to fit, but what did I know? To me, she looked like a beautiful name and Janet was a waste on her. All the Janets I knew were exhausting women with slight, secret drinking problems and held titles in the PTA. I wanted to rename her something better fitting to wash the bitter taste out of my mouth but knew I hadn't such power. It's not like I addressed her by name too often anyway other than the few times she'd pissed me off and I let the name Janet slice through the air with a sharp tongue. You can make any word a curse if you say it right.

Janet.

I wanted a cigarette but unfortunately smoking was "frowned upon" in therapy sessions. I'd never longed to be in the seventies more, I mean— the hairstyles were atrocious but I think I'd sacrifice my ideal of beauty for just one sweet drag. I brought the glass of cucumber water to my lips, buying time.

I don't know how the fuck it makes me feel—I thought in irritation to myself—*that's why I'm paying you ... so you can tell me how I feel.*

I tried to restructure that sentiment into a less offensive retort.

"If I knew how I felt, you'd be out of a job, miss," I said, half lowering the glass to speak and then raising it to my lips again. My face was hot and the contrast of the cool on my tongue was the only thing I was enjoying about this session. She feigned a laugh.

"Haha ... let's get serious and quit deflecting." She let her beautiful, piercing almond gaze fall on me like her white silk blouse fell on her frame. Gentle and soft, but with an edge.

She tucked her posh A-line cut behind her ears, making the gold and diamond drop earrings shimmer in the natural light. She looked like she belonged on a reality TV show, just dripping with class.

I, on the other hand, looked like a disaster.

I typically dressed how I felt, or how I wanted to feel and didn't have a hard time turning heads on my best days. But just the thought of going to therapy made me feel dreadful and since it was her fault I had to feel this way, I decided I wouldn't do her the favor of making myself presentable in the slightest. If I had to be torn into pieces for an hour, then I was going to look the part.

"I'm not deflecting!" She took off her glasses and set them on the table with a stern look.

"The humor? Cut it. It's deflecting and you're paying by the hour as you like to often remind me so let's cut the shit."

I liked that she felt comfortable enough to say shit in front of me. Made her seem more real. I couldn't stand the stuffy, inhuman holier-than-thou vibe that frequented my extensive list of the therapists I had terminated services with.

I realized pretty quickly that most mental health professionals were unqualified to sort through my particular brand of fucked up. I didn't have much hope for this one either but I had to try. I had created a beautiful life for myself and the skeletons of my past would pop out at the most inopportune times and leave me cleaning up yet another mess, and something had to be done if I wasn't to spend the rest of my life chasing my tail.

She repeated the question dry but firm as if to say she was gonna get an acceptable answer out of me whether I liked it or not. Almost like she saw me as a challenge and it excited her.

"How does that make you feel?" I was slow to respond but the words came out of my mouth without first presenting themselves in my mind to judge so that was a sure sign of it being the truth.

"I *feel* ..." I dragged the words out with a slight air of sarcasm. Just enough to be slightly defiant but not enough to be worth chastising. "Like it'd be in my best interest to take all of this to the grave."

"All of it?" she questioned, her face emotionless.

Poker face this woman.

I had learned how to read energy, body language and facial expressions as a survival tactic. I was quite talented. I'd even go as far as to call it an art form. She gave me nothing. Probably for the best. Nothing was always better than reading something I didn't want to see. It was probably the reason I was still here. Looks of shock and quiet shivers aren't exactly the thing you like to see when engaging with a professional and I'd seen my share.

"Um ... well you've heard my story. Which part did you think was a good conversation starter?" I couldn't help it. Turns out she was right. I did deflect with sarcasm. But I was answering her questions so she let it slide.

"Keta, you know what they say ... you're only as sick as your secrets." Concern filled her voice and though it seemed genuine, I let it roll off her tongue and then off of my back.

"What are you even talking about? I'm telling you! As we speak! I think that's the single criteria for it not being a secret, but correct me if I'm wrong." She swerved around my bullshit without missing a beat.

"I don't count. My job is to hold secrets. I'm legally bound. Anything you can't openly talk about without feeling shame is something you haven't made peace with so ... that's what this is. Making peace with it. So you can realize that it's too heavy to carry with you. This, Kate." Her hand made a pass through the air, indicating me and all of my surrounding bullshit. "This is heavy shit. And either you put it down or it slows you down. Your choice. But being that you're here voluntarily, I assume you want to put it down. I just don't think you know how. That's what we're doing here. Together. But you gotta help me out. This is more you than me and it sucks that after years of suffering at the hands of others, that you have to dig all this stuff up again and relive it but if it means that it will be the last time, don't you think that's worth giving a real chance?"

Fucking stupid sense-making lady.

I wanted to kick her and hug her at the same time. I took a deep breath as she asked the question again.

"How does that make you feel?" She gave me a nod and a look that said "you can do this" and then settled back into her chair with a notepad in her lap and a pen in her hand that was itching to jot down any note of substance.

"I—I guess it makes me feel—" I tried to hold back my tears, to which she cut me off.

"Let it come. Don't fight it. Continue—"

"It makes me feel like if anyone knew the truth, that it would be impossible to love me." I let the tears flow freely.

"Would you find someone you loved less valuable if they had been through the things you have been through?" Her question stung. I knew where this was going and I didn't want to go there but I let go and let it happen.

"No … I would love them the same. But I'm not like everybody—"

"You don't know what all the other people are like. And I'm assuming you being so guarded, you actually have a more limited view and experience. How can you know when you never let anyone get that close?"

"Well I have with a few," I said, wiping tears off the bridge of my nose.

"And—" she inquired expectantly. I shrugged.

"Ehhh—mixed reviews."

"But the ones that accept you wholly, was it worth the risk of the few who didn't to have those few that do?"

Good question. Touché psyche lady. Touché.

"Umm … yeah … don't know what I'd do without them."

"So all in all, you'd say it's been a positive experience?"

"With them," I replied. "Emphasis on *them.*"

"But they're the only ones that matter …" The room fell silent and I thought about it for a moment before she continued.

"Do you think that your fear of not being loved or feeling unworthiness of love is really a projection on to other people of how you feel about yourself?" My facial expression was unamused. Why did this conversation rip me open to the core? They were just words and yet they felt like daggers as she continued.

"What if the only power this held over you was the power that you gave it?"

"So you're saying it's all in my head?" My defenses raised again, always ready at a moment's notice.

"No … that's not what I'm saying at all. But if it were …"

"If it were what?" I was growing impatient and frustrated, shedding all of my layers of protection and being laid bare. I felt vulnerable and despite all that I had been through, vulnerable was the worst thing that I had ever felt.

"If it were, you'd have the power to change it." It clicked, the Rubik's Cube finally flush in order on all sides. I held back slightly, almost afraid of my own power.

"I get it, and you're right … you are. But it's not that simple." She nodded softly, her expression one of understanding and relief. She was getting somewhere, however gently she needed to tread.

"Walk me through that phrase."

"Which phrase?"

"It's not that simple."

I took a deep breath and absorbed the supportive energy in the room, reminding myself for the tenth time that hour that I was safe, and spoke.

"In my mind … In my mind, if people knew the truth, they'd whisper and stare whenever I walked into a room. 'She's the one,' they'd say. They'd say if they were me, they'd have found a better way out, philosophizing my tragedies with no point of reference. Conclude that I chose the path I was strewn down, mind you, a path I'd need to retrace on multiple occasions, picking up the pieces of myself cast along it to assemble the semblance of human being that sits in front of you now. The self that can't stand to hear the whispers behind the French tips of the gap donning horror shows that hide their evil and judgments behind a facade of cause or religion. They think they're better."

"Are they?" She had leaned in, deeply captivated by my honesty.

"Better? No … They just had better. I'd bet my life that had they had even one card of mine in their deck, they'd have folded like lawn chairs. Yet here I am doing better than them."

"And what would you say to them if they were here now?" I paused only for an instant before a weight-lifting smile crowded my face as I replied.

"I'd say fuck them … and fuck *that* … the only way they'd know what it took to survive my life was if they were me and they aren't. So as far as I'm concerned, they can take their opinions and fuck right off." Janet let a chuckle escape from behind her pursed lips as I continued. "They were born into a game where they got to pick between state schools and I got my pick of state prisons. The goal of their game was to get married, paint their picket fence white and duplicate their genes. The goal of mine was to survive."

"And what does that mean?" She couldn't hide her eagerness as she beckoned me forward to the finish line.

279

"What does what mean?" I said, stopping just short.

"If the goal of your game was to survive, what does that mean for you?" she said starry-eyed, pointing at me with her pen for emphasis. I felt a peace enter me that I had never known.

Tears, endless tears joined together, etching a creek bed into my cheeks. She beamed with pride nudging me there again.

"Say it," she said softly, reaching for my hand and grasping it tight in hers.

"It means …," I said, "it means … I won."

"You did," she said, nodding as I closed my eyes and internalized that statement, trying to hold on to the feeling just a moment longer. She interrupted as expected and my eyes fluttered open, taking in her next words.

"What would you say to ten-year-old Keta, or fifteen-year-old Keta? The little girl that's going through all of this?" We had just gotten to a space of relief and she wanted to dive back into the hurt. I let the frustration wash over me and let it go as soon as it came. It would do me no good here. I stuttered as I regained my composure.

"I'd tell her that she was safe … even if she didn't feel like it and … it was gonna be hard for a bit and she was going to want to give up but she can't …"

"Why … why can't she give up?" She pushed me forward.

"Because one day … she was going to make herself really proud … and if she gave up … if I … if I gave up … I'd miss out on such a beautiful life." I took the tissue from Janet's outstretched hand and held it tight in my white knuckles at my knee.

I kinda liked how the tears felt. Like an exorcism. Cleansing. I left them to rest on my cheeks.

They had earned the right to that place today.

"Is that today?" she asked, leaning back in her chair. I could have sworn she looked proud for a moment but it was just a flash before it vanished into her honey eyes.

"Is what today?" I asked

"The day when you made yourself proud."

I looked off the eaves of my mind at all I had achieved, not only in the physical world but in the ether. The woman who looked back at me in the mirror. The one with the heart that refused to harden into an icy block no matter the storms it had weathered. The one with the smile that lit up a room and the eyes that danced with flame. The one that wore her scars like tattoos. Comfortable in her skin, therefore, allowing others to do the same. A woman not crowded by judgments of others and a spirit that flew freely through life like a honey bee from flower to flower, pollinating along the way.

The published model, songwriter and poet.

The sister, the auntie and the friend.

You'd never know what she'd been through by looking at her. Even your wildest guesses couldn't come close to knowing what darkness she'd seen. Because how could a light so bright even know what the darkness was?

That's who I wanted to be. But for one to be a true light, they must first survive the darkness.

I did. I won. Was today the day that I would finally be proud of her? Was it?

I looked at Janet with a small smile, took one more cleansing breath, and replied.

"Yes."

About the Author

Keta Loren is an influencer turned advocate with over 500,000 social media followers. A life-long creator, Keta Loren is a published song writer, model and author. As a survivor of abuse, the foster care system, human trafficking and addiction, she views it as her responsibility to use her platform to share her story and help others.

Instagram @iamketamusik

TikTok @ketaloren

Website ketaloren.com

Made in the USA
Las Vegas, NV
24 September 2021

31056555R00157